THE DIABETES DOUBLE-QUICK COOKBOOK

THE
Diabetes
Double-Quick
COOKBOOK
2ND EDITION

BY BETTY MARKS

SURREY BOOKS
Chicago

THE DIABETES DOUBLE-QUICK COOKBOOK, 2nd Edition, is published by Surrey Books, Inc., 230 E. Ohio St., Suite 120, Chicago, IL 60611.

Second edition: 1 2 3 4 5

This book is manufactured in the United States of America.

Library of Congress Cataloging-in-Publication Data

Marks, Betty.
   The diabetes double-quick cookbook / by Betty Marks.—2nd ed.
      p. cm.
   Includes index.
   Previous ed. published under the title: The microwave diabetes cookbook.
   ISBN 1-57284-039-0
   1. Diabetes—Diet therapy—Recipes. 2. Microwave cookery. I. Marks, Betty. Microwave diabetes cookbook. II. Title.

   RC662.M345 2002
   641.5'6314–dc21

                                                          2002022153

For prices on quantity purchases or for a free book catalog, contact Surrey Books at the above address.

Distributed to the trade by Publishers Group West

To all those who enjoy the dance of life and want to cook healthful meals quickly.

Acknowledgments

Testing and tasting new foods is always an experience—sometimes agreeable, other times not so great. My warm thanks for doing this go to two of my favorite cooks, Nancy Henderson and Nancy Racusin.

My gratitude is also extended to the many friends and neighbors who willingly ate my dishes, mostly with glee, often with lucid commentary. These include Cindy and Jeff Brody, Jane Brody and Richard Engquist, Fran Korein and Ray Belsky, Helen and Norman Stern, Eleanor and Marc Anderson, and Bernice and Earl Balis.

I am especially grateful to Dr. Daniel Lorber of the Diabetes Control Foundation for his prefatory remarks, and to the indispensable Hope Warshaw, M.M.Sc., R.D., and Linda Yoakam, R.D., M.S., for their careful and accurate nutritional analyses.

Contents

Foreword

My life is full—there is hardly enough time in the day to accomplish everything, especially since I have diabetes. From work to activities such as swimming, distance walking, exercise, art, theater, dance, and tango, little time is left to shop for food, prepare it and turn it into delicious dishes. But thanks to the microwave oven, one can cook quickly and still taste life's many offerings.

Since switching to a microwave for my food preparation I decided to share the kind of heart healthy cooking with others who have diabetes or need to watch their food intake carefully for other reasons. The microwave cooks without fat, and vegetables do not lose their benefits as in a pot of water. Bread, cakes, and muffins can be baked in the microwave. Foods cooked in a microwave retain their nutrients and stay hotter longer.

In addition to cutting down cooking time, using the microwave eliminates the need to scrub pots since food may be cooked in the very dish on which it will be served. Time saved allows one to pursue whatever activities are preferred to kitchen duty, whether work or pleasure. Children can learn to use the microwave safely and easily.

It is my hope that by using these fast but delicious recipes my readers will enjoy well-balanced, tasty, and attractive meals in minutes and spend the time saved in pursuits that bring them contentment.

— Betty Marks
New York City

Preface

People with diabetes have a primary concern in their daily lives. Staying in good control requires constant vigilance in many aspects of every day's chores and pleasures. Eating at regular times, and sometimes in between, exercising, and balancing insulin intake with energy expenditure is a full-time task.

Good nutrition is another major concern for those who want to keep trim and stay as healthy as possible even though they lead busy lives. Very often, food is needed in a hurry. Betty Marks, who fills her life with many activities, addresses this dilemma in this cookbook. The microwave has proved a boon to her in the preparation of more than one hundred healthful recipes.

As a person whose life depends upon several daily doses of insulin, Betty has developed a way to make many marvelous meals! And in *The Diabetes Double-Quick Cookbook* she shares these fast and simple methods with all of you whose needs are as demanding as her own.

All too often in the past, family and friends have not wanted to eat the same food that the family member with diabetes has selected. But we now know that everyone can benefit from a heart-healthy diet—one that is low in fat, cholesterol, and sodium, is moderate in calories, and does not contain the empty calories of sugar and honey.

The recipes chosen for inclusion in *The Diabetes Double-Quick Cookbook* range from appetizers, soups, fish, meat and poultry, grains and vegetables, pastas, sauces, baked breads and muffins to desserts. They are all simple to prepare and fast to cook. Everyone can enjoy the good taste and speed of these recipes that satisfy the appetite *and* the need to eat correctly.

With this book's culinary contributions, the management of diabetes mellitus becomes more agreeable and, because of the vast time saving, an opportunity to lead a more enjoyable and richer life.

> — Daniel Louis Lorber, M.D., F.A.C.P.
> Associate Clinical Professor of Medicine,
> Cornell University Medical College, New York City;
> Director, Division of Endocrinology at New York Hospital,
> Medical Center of Queens, New York City;
> Medical Director, Diabetes Control Foundation, New York City

Introduction

A quick, easy, tasty recipe repertory for people with diabetes? Sounds impossible! Yet once again Betty Marks has created such a collection of recipes, chock full of interesting food combinations and unique ingredient mixtures. These recipes will help turn the rigor of daily meal planning into an interesting adventure with food. Best yet, these recipes are quick and easy because they're all microwavable. Thus, they go hand-in-hand with today's fast-paced lifestyle.

"Dull," "boring," "repetitive," "lacks zip"—as a registered dietitian, these are words I often hear to describe eating the foods and meals you can eat when you have diabetes. Unfortunately, this perspective leads many people to stray from healthier eating. To maximize adherence to a diabetes meal plan—and thus to improve management of diabetes—it's essential to master the art of integrating both taste and zip into daily food preparation.

Today's recommendations for diabetes nutrition management, simply stated, are a call for healthy eating. The same nutrition and eating guidelines steering diabetes meal planning are those touted loud and clear for all Americans: eat less fat, saturated fat, cholesterol, and protein; more starches and fiber; and limited sweets. These goals are rigorously kept in focus in *The Diabetes Double-Quick Cookbook*.

To further guide the meal-maker in this quest for sound nutrition, each recipe includes nutritional data, stating per-serving total calories and amounts of dietary fiber, sodium, cholesterol, carbohydrates, protein, and fat—saturated, polyunsaturated, and monounsaturated. These values were derived using the computer program "Recipe Analysis and Exchange List Conversion" developed by Lawrence Wheeler, M.D., Ph.D., and Madelyn Wheeler, M.S., R.D., C.D.E. Nutrition information in this program relies mainly on United States Department of Agriculture figures.

Along with the nutritional evaluation, each recipe also provides diabetes exchange calculations. The exchange system, developed by The American Dietetic Association and The American Diabetes Association, assists people with diabetes in meal planning. The food exchanges provided here were determined according to recommended guidelines of The American Diabetes Association.

To sum up, Betty Marks proves once again in this cookbook that diabetes management, healthy eating, fast and easy preparation, and tasty meals can harmoniously coexist on the same dinner plate.

— **Hope S. Warshaw**, M.M.Sc., R.D., C.D.E.
Author, *The Restaurant Companion—A Guide to Healthier Eating Out*

Microwave Hints

How to Use the Microwave

▲ Consult the manufacturer's instructions and learn the wattage of your microwave.

▲ Most microwave recipes, including those in this book, are developed for 600–700-watt ovens. If your microwave has fewer than 600 watts, adjust the cooking times as follows:
- 500 to 600 watts: add 15 seconds to every minute of cooking time specified.
- 400 to 500 watts: add 30 seconds to every minute of cooking time specified in recipe.
- If your microwave is less than 500 watts, use "High" setting even when directions call for 50 percent power.

It is better to undercook food since it can always be returned to the oven for additional time. Check meat, poultry, fish, and vegetables for doneness by piercing with a fork.

The size of the microwave oven is relative to the wattage: the higher the wattage, the larger the microwave. If measuring containers suggested in recipes do not fit in your microwave, use smaller bowls, cups, etc., in multiples.

▲ For cooking muffins and breads at altitudes of 3,500 feet and above, use larger pans and fill only halfway. Use more liquid and cook longer than the specified time. Elevate the baking dish on an inverted saucer.

▲ Power levels:
- High-100%
- Medium High-70%
- Medium-50%
- Medium Low or Defrost-30%
- Low-10%

▲ For the visually impaired, Braille overlays are available from microwave manufacturers.

▲ Use only microwave-safe plates or dishes. Any non-metal dish; glass or ceramic casserole; Pyrex measuring cup, pie plate, or loaf pan may be used. Round or oval dishes are the best for even cooking.

▲ Paper plates, towels, wax paper, and plastic wrap may be used in the microwave. Covering foods with wax paper or plastic wrap helps steam food while keeping it moist and preventing splattering.

▲ To vent plastic wrap, pierce with a knife or fold under one side. Do not use plastic wrap if cooking for long periods of time, and try not to let heated plastic wrap come in contact with food. When removing plastic wrap or wax paper from heated dishes, peel off away from you to avoid steam burns.

▲ Do not use recycled paper towels or bags.

▲ Use pot holders when removing dishes from the microwave.

▲ Do not use the microwave with the door open; most models will not operate with the door open.

▲ Before starting to cook, read the recipe carefully and assemble all ingredients, placing them on the kitchen counter in order of their use. To save more time, keep the larder stocked by reviewing meal plans for the week ahead and shopping for the required ingredients.

▲ Do not use plastic containers such as margarine or butter tubs in the microwave, as they may melt at high temperatures.

▲ Aluminum foil may be used around edges of cooking dishes, but metal pans should not be used; all metals should be kept away from sides of the oven.

▲ Learn about microwaves; microwaves are short radio waves that penetrate food, starting on the outer layer and moving inward gradually. They cause food molecules to move, producing friction. This makes heat that cooks food. Microwaves penetrate food from all directions, and the heating takes place in the food itself. No heat is produced in the oven, which keeps the kitchen cool. Microwaves do not change the chemical composition of food, they are not harmful, and there is no danger of radiation.

▲ To clean the microwave oven: place a small bowl of water in the microwave, and heat on High for 2 minutes or until water boils. Remove water and wipe clean.

▲ Microwave ovens are great time-savers, but they are accessories. They are not appropriate for cooking all foods. They are not recommended for browning and crisping food nor for roasting chickens, turkey, or beef. The microwave is superb for cooking vegetables, fish, stews, soups, casseroles, chicken and turkey chunks, and quick breads and muffins. Since the microwave extracts one-third more fat from meat than a conventional oven while holding in other juices, it benefits people who want moist, low-fat foods.

Cooking Tips

- ▲ Standing Time: recipes often call for some additional cooking that takes place after dish is removed from the oven.
- ▲ Vegetables can be cooked in the microwave while another dish is "standing."
- ▲ Partially freeze meat or poultry (about 30 minutes) for easier slicing.
- ▲ Do not refreeze meats thawed in microwave, and do not partially cook food.
- ▲ Small pieces of meat and poultry cook faster than large chunks, thin portions faster than thick, and small quantities of food cook faster than large quantities. Deboned meat or poultry cooks faster and more evenly.
- ▲ Do not leave food in the microwave for more than two hours.
- ▲ Stir foods in mid-cycle or several times for even cooking. Move undercooked food to outside of dish and pieces that are done to the center.
- ▲ Rotate cooking dish unless your microwave is equipped with a turntable. Wind-up turntables may be purchased for use in the microwave oven.
- ▲ Turn over large foods such as squash, eggplant, and potatoes in mid-cycle for even cooking.
- ▲ Arrange uniform meat or poultry pieces in a single layer or circle, leaving center empty.
- ▲ To get more juice from a lemon or orange, heat in microwave for half a minute or so before squeezing.
- ▲ Elevate cooking dishes when called for (as in some baked recipes) on an inverted saucer. This allows microwaves to circulate under the dish and cook more evenly.

▲ To toast nuts and seeds, place on a 9-inch glass pie plate and cook on High for 1 to 2 minutes, shaking the dish once. Pine nuts (pignoli), sunflower or pumpkin seeds, and sesame seeds may be toasted this way. Cover with paper towels to avoid popping. Nuts such as walnuts, almonds, filberts, and pecans may be toasted the same way but without covering. Add a generous shake of cinnamon to the nuts for flavor.

Special Utensils

▲ In addition to 1- and 2-cup measures, larger microwave-safe measures are also recommended, and they are available in sizes from 1 to 5 quarts. Casseroles and baking dishes also come in these sizes.

▲ 8- to 9-inch glass and ceramic pie plates are very useful.

▲ For baking muffins, a plastic microwave-safe muffin tin is helpful. However, if this is difficult to find, I recommend using paper hot cups (unwaxed) cut down about halfway. They may then be filled partially with muffin mixture and baked in the microwave safely.

▲ Browning dishes are available, made by Corning and other manufacturers. Follow directions for first heating the dish. (Mine is heated with the oven on High for 5 minutes.) When the recipe calls for browning fish, chicken, or beef, place slices on the heated dish and return to the oven. Care should be taken when removing the dish from the oven, as it will be quite hot.

▲ Probes and thermometers are useful to determine doneness.

Appetizers

Many people enjoy sitting down with a few nibbles before having their main meal. Others like to graze as a style of eating—tasting a variety of small dishes rather than eating one large entree. Here are a variety of offerings, all of which are tasty and truly appetizing, that will satisfy either desire.

Blue Corn Crisps

Serves: 4 (4 per serving)
Cooking time: 1 minute
Preparation time: 2 minutes

> 16 blue corn tortilla chips
> ¼ cup low-fat mozzarella or cheese substitute, shredded
> 2 tablespoons mild salsa

Line platter with wax paper and arrange tortilla chips over it. Sprinkle grated cheese over each chip and top with a dab of sauce. Microwave on High just until cheese melts, about 1 minute. Serve while warm.

Per Serving: 4 Chol (mg); 9 Carbo (g); 3 Prot (g); 201 Na (mg)
Dietary Fiber: 1.5 g **Fat (g):** 4; Sat 1.4; Poly 1.3; Mono .8 **Calories:** 78
Exchanges: ½ starch/bread; 1 fat

Clam Dip

Serves: 8 (2-tablespoon servings)
Cooking time: 1 minute
Preparation time: 5 minutes

¼ cup low-fat cottage cheese
¼ cup Yogurt Sour Cream (see index)
1 6½-ounce can minced clams, drained
1 tablespoon shallots, minced
1 teaspoon horseradish
   Dash tabasco sauce or cayenne pepper

Whip cottage cheese and Yogurt Sour Cream in blender until smooth. Add remaining ingredients, blend, and place in 2-cup microwave-safe measure. Microwave on Medium (50%) 1 minute, stirring once. Serve warm or chilled with blue corn chips or crudites.

Per Serving: 16 Chol (mg); 2 Carbo (g); 7 Prot (g); 56 Na (mg)
Dietary Fiber: 0 **Fat (g):** 1; Sat .1; Poly .1; Mono 4 **Calories:** 44
Exchanges: 1 lean meat
Calculation does not include chips or vegetables.

Hot Bean Dip

Serves: 4 (2-tablespoon servings)
Cooking time: 2 minutes
Preparation time: 5 minutes

1 8-ounce can of kidney or pinto beans, rinsed and drained
2 cloves garlic, minced
¼ cup shallots, chopped
½ cup tofu (bean curd)
1 medium stalk celery, chopped
2 tablespoons mild salsa
2 tablespoons part-skim mozzarella cheese, grated
Parsley, chopped, for garnish

Mix all ingredients except last two in blender or food processor and puree. Place in 16-ounce microwave-safe glass bowl, and microwave on High for 1 minute. Remove, stir to mix, sprinkle with cheese, and return to microwave on High for another 40 seconds, just until cheese melts. Garnish with sprinkle of chopped parsley. Serve as dip with vegetable crudites.

Per Serving: 5 Chol (mg); 13 Carbo (g); 8 Prot (g); 373 Na (mg)
Dietary Fiber: 2.7 g **Fat (g):** 3; Sat 1.1; Poly .9; Mono .7 **Calories:** 109
Exchanges: 1 starch/bread; ½ lean meat

Pepper Pizza

Serves: 4
Cooking time: 7 minutes
Preparation time: 10 minutes

4 6-inch corn tortillas
1 teaspoon olive oil
2 cloves garlic, minced
½ medium green bell pepper, julienned
½ medium red bell pepper, julienned
½ cup fresh mushrooms, sliced
¼ cup tomato puree
Oregano
2 tablespoons part-skim mozzarella (or no-fat cheese substitute), grated

Place tortillas in oven and microwave on High for 3 minutes until crisp. Remove from oven and set aside. Place olive oil in small glass bowl with garlic and peppers. Microwave on High for 2 minutes.

Mix in tomato puree, oregano, and sliced mushrooms, and microwave for 1½ minutes more. Spread on top of tortillas, and sprinkle with cheese. Place tortillas on serving dish and microwave for 30 to 40 seconds until cheese melts.

Per Serving: 5 Chol (mg); 17 Carbo (g); 5 Prot (g); 158 Na (mg)
Dietary Fiber: 1.8 g **Fat (g):** 4; Sat 1.1; Poly .2; Mono 1.2 **Calories:** 115
Exchanges: ½ starch/bread; 1 vegetable; 1 fat

Potato Cheese Chips

Serves: 4 (4 slices per serving)
Cooking time: 8½ to 10½ minutes
Preparation time: 5 minutes plus chilling time

> 2 medium Idaho potatoes, about 1 pound
>
> 2 ounces low-fat shredded cheese—Alpine Lace, part skim mozzarella, etc.
>
> ¼ teaspoon each of garlic powder, chili powder, and dried basil
>
> Dash of pepper to taste

Wash potatoes and prick each with a fork. Wrap each potato in microwave-safe paper towel and place end-to-end in oven. Microwave on High for 4 to 5 minutes. Turn potatoes over and microwave on High another 4 to 5 minutes. Unwrap, let cool, and refrigerate.

When chilled, cut into ¼-inch slices and top with sprinkling of cheese, a dusting of combined spices, and dash of pepper.

Line oven with paper towels and arrange potato slices on them. Microwave for 30 to 40 seconds, just until cheese melts. Makes 16 slices.

Per Serving: 8 Chol. (mg); 13 Carbo (g); 5 Prot (g); 72 Na (mg)
Dietary Fiber: 1.8 g **Fat (g):** 2; Sat 1.5; Poly .1; Mono .6 **Calories:** 91
Exchanges: 1 starch/bread

Sesame Chick Pea Dip

Serves: 8 (2-tablespoon servings)
Cooking time: 1½ minutes
Preparation time: 5 minutes

- 1 cup canned chick peas (garbanzos), rinsed and drained
- 2 tablespoons lemon juice
- 1 tablespoon tahini (sesame paste) or peanut butter
- ⅛ teaspoon cayenne
- 3 tablespoons water (or more to thin)
- 1 teaspoon toasted sesame seeds
- 1 teaspoon parsley, chopped

In a food processor fitted with a steel blade, blend together all ingredients but the last two. Turn into a 12-ounce glass dish and microwave on High for 1½ minutes, stirring mid-cycle. Remove, stir again to mix, and sprinkle with garnish of sesame seeds and parsley. Serve as dip with pita crisps or vegetable crudites.

Per Serving: 0 Chol (mg); 8 Carbo (g); 3 Prot (g); 14 Na (mg)
Dietary Fiber: 2.9 g **Fat (g):** 1; Sat .3; Poly .7; Mono .7 **Calories:** 60
Exchanges: ½ starch/bread

Stuffed Mushroom Caps

Serves: 6 (2 mushrooms per serving)
Cooking time: 2 to 3 minutes
Preparation time: 10 minutes

12	large mushrooms, cleaned
½	cup onion, finely chopped
¼	cup whole wheat breadcrumbs
1	teaspoon lemon juice
2	tablespoons part skim ricotta
1	teaspoon Dijon mustard
	Dashes cumin, turmeric, celery seed, and poppy seed
	Salt and pepper to taste
	Paprika
	Parsley, chopped, for garnish

Remove stems from mushrooms and chop. Mix stems with onions, breadcrumbs, and lemon juice. Combine with all remaining ingredients except paprika and parsley, and stuff mushroom caps with mixture. Place stuffed caps on serving platter, dust with paprika, and microwave on High for 2 to 3 minutes. Sprinkle chopped parsley on each mushroom and serve warm or chilled.

Per Serving: 1 Chol (mg); 5 Carbo (g); 2 Prot (g); 66 Na (mg)
Dietary Fiber: 1.7 g **Fat (g):** 1; Sat .39; Poly .1; Mono .2 **Calories:** 3
Exchanges: 1 vegetable

Soup

Soup is a splendid way to start a meal, or indeed can be a major part of the meal itself. The soups in this section are simple to prepare, and with the microwave and food processor take just minutes to cook. Many use fresh vegetables, some use nutritious beans, and the addition of non-fat milk or yogurt adds an extra bit of calcium. Spices, seasonings, and garnishes provide appealing tastes and colors. Chopped parsley, paprika, diced bell peppers, or shredded carrots lend texture as toppings, too.

When transferring hot liquid to the blender or food processor, use only small amounts at a time and let cool a little before blending. The pureed soup can always be returned to the microwave oven for rewarming.

Cauliflower Soup

Serves: 4
Cooking time: 10 to 11 minutes
Preparation time: 10 minutes

1 pound cauliflower, trimmed, cut into florets
1 medium carrot, scraped and diced
1 stalk celery with leaves, sliced
½ onion, sliced
1 teaspoon Vogue chicken-base flavor mixed with ½ cup water
2 cups water
¼ cup non-fat dry milk
1 teaspoon curry powder
1 teaspoon caraway seeds
½ teaspoon red pepper flakes
  Salt and pepper to taste
  Juice of ½ lemon
  Parsley for garnish
  Dash paprika

Place cauliflower, carrot, celery, onion, and water and flavoring in a 2-quart measure. Microwave on High for 8 minutes, stirring once, until cauliflower stems are soft. Let cool a few minutes, and place in blender or food processor with 2 cups of water (as needed to thin) and puree. Add milk and curry powder and process for a few seconds.

Return to measure, stir in caraway seeds, red pepper flakes, and salt and pepper to taste. Microwave about 2 to 3 minutes to warm. Stir in lemon juice, and garnish with parsley and dash of paprika.

Per Serving: 1 Chol (mg); 11 Carbo (g); 4 Prot (g); 75 Na (mg)
Dietary Fiber: 3.5 g **Fat (g):** 0; Sat .1; Poly .2; Mono .1 **Calories:** 57
Exchanges: 2 vegetable

Chicken Broth

Serves: 12 (1-cup servings)
Cooking time: 30 minutes
Preparation time: 10 minutes

1 broiler chicken, cut up, or 2 pounds chicken parts
4 cloves garlic
2 stalks celery with tops, chopped coarsely
6 parsley sprigs
1 bay leaf
6 peppercorns
2 medium onions, quartered
2 carrots, cut in half
1 parsnip, cut in half
3 quarts water

Place all ingredients in a 5-quart measure or casserole and cover with vented plastic wrap. Microwave on High for 15 minutes. Skim off any foam that accumulates. Re-cover and microwave on Medium (50%) for 15 minutes, still skimming off any froth.

Strain stock into a bowl and let cool to room temperature. Discard solids, or give the cooked chicken meat to the cat. Cool stock in refrigerator, and discard fat that congeals on surface. Place stock in small containers and freeze for future use. Makes 3 quarts.

Per Serving: 0 Chol (mg); 4 Carbo (g); 1 Prot (g); 10 Na (mg)
Dietary Fiber: 0 **Fat (g):** 0; Sat 0; Poly 0; Mono 0 **Calories:** 20
Exchanges: Free

Creamy Carrot Soup

Serves: 4
Cooking time: 11 to 12 minutes
Preparation time: 10 minutes

2 teaspoons canola oil
1 teaspoon whole wheat flour
2 cups carrots, scraped and sliced
2 cups Chicken Broth (see previous recipe)
Pinch salt
¼ teaspoon dried thyme
1 bay leaf
½ teaspoon fresh ginger root, chopped
2 teaspoons frozen orange juice concentrate
½ teaspoon dried tarragon
Fresh pepper to taste
1 cup skim milk
¼ cup non-fat dry milk
Few sprigs fresh mint or ½ teaspoon dried mint; or fresh parsley for garnish

Mix first 8 ingredients in a 2-quart measure. Microwave for 10 minutes on High. Let cool a few minutes. Discard bay leaf and turn into food processor or blender a little at a time. Process to blend.

Add orange juice, tarragon, pepper, and milk and blend. Return to original container and microwave on High for 1 to 2 minutes until warmed through. Top with garnish of mint or parsley. May also be served chilled.

Per Serving: 2 Chol (mg); 15 Carbo (g); 5 Prot (g); 109 Na (mg)
Dietary Fiber: 1.9g **Fat (g):** 2; Sat .4; Poly .2; Mono 1.6 **Calories:** 97
Exchanges: 2 vegetable; ½ skim milk

Crunchy Vegetable Soup

Serves: 4
Cooking time: 11 to 14 minutes
Preparation time: 10 minutes

1½ cups asparagus, about 6 spears
1 medium carrot, finely chopped
1 stalk celery, finely chopped
2 tablespoons onion, chopped
2 medium mushrooms, sliced
1 cup Chicken Broth (see index)
1 cup non-fat plain yogurt
Dash tarragon
Dash cayenne
Pepper to taste
Diced pimentos for garnish

Place asparagus spears on dish with a little water and cover with wax paper. Microwave on High for 5 to 6 minutes. Cut into 1-inch pieces and place in food processor with vegetables and chicken broth. Process until mixed.

Turn into 8-cup measure and microwave on High for 6 to 8 minutes until soup simmers. Stir in yogurt. Serve with dusting of tarragon, cayenne, and pepper and a garnish of diced pimentos.

May be served warm or chilled. Any combination of vegetables may be used for this potage—broccoli, cauliflower, cucumbers, radishes—just as long as they are crunchable.

Per Serving: 2 Chol (mg); 9 Carbo (g); 5 Prot (g); 63 Na (mg)
Dietary Fiber: 2.5g **Fat (g):** 1; Sat .4; Poly .3; Mono .2 **Calories:** 55
Exchanges: 2 vegetable

Egg Drop Soup

Serves: 4
Cooking time: 9 to 11 minutes
Preparation time: 5 minutes

    4 cups Chicken Broth (see index)
    ¼ cup scallions, sliced
    ½ cup frozen peas and mushrooms
    1 tablespoon fresh ginger root, finely minced
    2 teaspoons low-sodium soy sauce
    2 eggs, one yolk only, well beaten

Pour the broth into a 6-cup casserole or measure and cover with vented plastic wrap. Microwave on High for 8 to 10 minutes, until broth boils. Add scallions, peas and mushrooms, ginger root, and soy sauce. Microwave on High another 1 minute. Uncover and slowly drizzle egg into the soup, using a circular motion.

Per Serving: 70 Chol (mg); 6 Carbo (g); 4 Prot (g); 141 Na (mg)
Dietary Fiber: 1.0g **Fat (g):** 2; Sat .5; Poly .3; Mono .6 **Calories:** 43
Exchanges: 1 vegetable

Garden Green Soup

Serves: 4
Cooking time: 6 to 8 minutes
Preparation time: 15 minutes

- 1 teaspoon canola oil
- 4 shallots, sliced
- 3 cloves garlic, minced
- 4 cups mixed greens, rinsed well and shredded (use combination of romaine and red leaf or Boston lettuce, spinach, escarole, and sorrel)
- 2 cups skim milk
- 1 cup Chicken Broth (see index)
- 1 tablespoon oat bran
- ¼ cup fresh basil, chopped (or 1 teaspoon dried)
- Rind of 1 lemon, grated
- Pepper to taste

Place oil, shallots, and garlic in 2-quart measure, and microwave on High for 2 minutes. Add greens and stir to combine. Microwave on High for 2 to 3 minutes, stirring, until greens are wilted. Add remaining ingredients and transfer to a food processor, two cups at a time. Return to original container and microwave another 2 to 3 minutes to warm. Serve warm or chilled.

Per Serving: 2 Chol (mg); 11 Carbo (g); 6 Prot (g); 92 Na (mg)
Dietary Fiber: 2.4g **Fat (g):** 1; Sat .3; Poly .2; Mono .8 **Calories:** 79
Exchanges: 1 vegetable; ½ milk

Mexican Corn Soup

Serves: 4
Cooking time: 5 to 6 minutes
Preparation time: 10 minutes

> 1 carrot, shredded (about ½ cup)
> 1 medium green pepper, chopped (½ cup)
> ½ cup shallots, chopped
> 1 teaspoon vegetable oil
> 1 cup corn niblets (fresh, canned, or frozen and thawed)
> 2 cups Chicken Broth (see index)
> ½ cup non-fat dry milk mixed with enough water to make 1 cup
> ⅛ teaspoon red pepper flakes
> ¼ teaspoon celery seed

Place carrot, green pepper, and shallots in a 2-quart casserole or measure with the vegetable oil, and microwave on High for 3 minutes. Add remaining ingredients, and transfer and mix in a food processor or blender, a little at a time. Return to original container and microwave on High 2 to 3 minutes until warm, stirring once.

Per Serving: 3 Chol (mg); 19 Carbo (g); 5 Prot (g); 65 Na (mg)
Dietary Fiber: 2.5g **Fat (g):** 0; Sat 0; Poly 0; Mono 0 **Calories:** 91
Exchanges: 1 starch/bread; ½ milk

Snow Pea Soup

Serves: 4
Cooking time: 14 to 16 minutes
Preparation time: 15 minutes

- 4 cups Chicken Broth (see index)
- ¼ cup scallions, minced
- ¼ cup carrots, finely chopped
- 1 clove garlic, minced
- 1 teaspoon fresh ginger root, grated
- 1 teaspoon low-sodium soy sauce
- ¼ cup mushrooms, sliced
- 1 cup snow peas (about ¼ pound), washed and trimmed
- 4 ounces firm tofu (bean curd), cut into ½-inch cubes
- Scallions, additional, for garnish

Place broth, scallions, carrots, garlic, ginger root, and soy sauce in an 8-cup measure. Microwave on High for 8 to 10 minutes. Add mushrooms and cook 5 minutes more on High. Add snow peas and microwave for 1 minute more on High. Stir in tofu and garnish with scallions.

Per Serving: 0 Chol (mg); 8 Carbo (g); 4 Prot (g); 61 Na (mg)
Dietary Fiber: 1.3g **Fat (g):** 2; Sat .2; Poly .8; Mono .3 **Calories:** 39
Exchanges: 1½ vegetable

Squash Soup

Serves: 6 (1-cup servings)
Cooking time: 13 minutes
Preparation time: 10 to 13 minutes plus 15 minutes resting time

- 2 acorn or butternut squash, about 1 pound each
- ½ cup onion, chopped
- 2 cups Chicken Broth (see index)
- ½ teaspoon cinnamon, ground
- ¼ teaspoon coriander, ground
- ¼ teaspoon cumin, ground
- ½ teaspoon turmeric
- Fresh pepper to taste
- 1 tablespoon apple cider vinegar
- 1 cup buttermilk
- 4 tablespoons non-fat dry milk
- 1 tablespoon low-sodium soy sauce
- 1 tablespoon fresh parsley, chopped

Place whole squash in oven and microwave on High for 2 minutes. Pierce deeply several times with a fork. Microwave on High for 6 to 8 minutes more until soft, turning squash over and rotating twice. Let stand 5 minutes or until cool enough to handle. Slice squash in half, discard seeds, and scrape out pulp. There should be about 3 cups of pulp.

Let squash cool for 10 minutes; turn into a blender or food processor with the onion and chicken stock and puree. Transfer to an 8-cup measuring bowl and add spices, vinegar, milks, and soy sauce. Microwave for 2 to 3 minutes until soup simmers. Adjust seasoning and serve with a garnish of parsley.

Per Serving: 2 Chol (mg); 30 Carbo (g); 4 Prot (g); 168 Na (mg)
Dietary Fiber: 5.1g **Fat (g):** 1; Sat .3; Poly. 1; Mono. 1 **Calories:** 95
Exchanges: 1 ½ starch/bread; ½ milk

Tomato Vegetable Soup

Serves: 4
Cooking time: 5 to 6 minutes
Preparation time: 5 minutes

> 3 cups canned Italian plum tomatoes
> 1 tablespoon frozen apple juice concentrate
> 1 tablespoon scallions, minced (reserve green tops for garnish)
> 2 whole cloves
> 1 bay leaf
> ½ cup frozen peas, thawed
> ½ cup corn kernels (canned or, if frozen, thawed)
> Dash pepper

Puree tomatoes in blender or food processor, and turn into a 9-inch-deep glass bowl or soup tureen. Add apple juice, scallions, cloves, and bay leaf and cover with vented plastic wrap. Microwave on High for 2 minutes.

Remove plastic, stir, and add peas and corn. Cover and microwave on High for 3 to 4 minutes more until heated through. Remove bay leaf and cloves, stir, and garnish with remaining green scallions and dashes of pepper.

Per Serving: 0 Chol (mg) 16; Carbo (g) 3; Prot (g); 312 Na (mg)
Dietary Fiber: 3.6g **Fat (g):** 1; Sat .1; Poly .2; Mono .1 **Calories:** 75
Exchanges: 1 starch/bread

Vichyssoise

Serves: 4
Cooking time: 3 to 5 minutes
Preparation time: 12 minutes

  1 cup Chicken Broth (see index)
  1 cup potatoes, peeled and cubed
  1½ cups leeks, well washed, chopped
  2 cups skim milk
    Few dashes celery seed
  ½ teaspoon salt
    Dash fresh pepper
  1 tablespoon part-skim ricotta cheese
    Few dashes cayenne

Place broth, potatoes, and leeks in a food processor and blend to liquefy. Turn into a 2-quart measure, and microwave 3 to 5 minutes until vegetables are cooked. Place remaining ingredients in food processor, add cooked vegetables, and process again until smooth. Pour into a bowl and chill before serving. Top with dusting of cayenne.

As a variation, this may also be made with sweet potatoes.

Per Serving: 4 Chol (mg); 16 Carbo (g); 9 Prot (g); 187 Na (mg)
Dietary Fiber: 1.3g **Fat (g):** 1; Sat .5; Poly .3; Mono .4 **Calories:** 111
Exchanges: ½ skim milk; ½ starch/bread

White Bean Soup

Serves: 6
Cooking time: 14 to 16 minutes
Preparation time: 20 minutes

2 cups celery, chopped
3 scallions, chopped
3 cloves garlic, chopped
1 teaspoon canola oil
1 medium onion, chopped
2 15-ounce cans cannellini beans, drained, rinsed
2 tablespoons oat bran
3 allspice berries
1 cup Chicken Broth (see index)
1 cup water
Dash thyme
Dash cayenne
½ teaspoon dill weed
Juice of 1 lemon
Pepper to taste
Few sprigs fresh parsley for garnish

Place celery, scallions, garlic, oil, and onion in a 2-quart measure, and microwave on High for 3 minutes, stirring once. Add remaining ingredients except parsley, and microwave on High for 10 to 12 minutes more. Let cool a little and turn into food processor in small batches to puree. Return to microwave for 1 minute on High if necessary to rewarm. Garnish with parsley, and serve warm or chilled.

Per Serving: 0 Chol (mg); 30 Carbo (g); 11 Prot (g); 45 Na (mg)
Dietary Fiber: 7.3g **Fat (g):** 1; Sat .3; Poly .2; Mono .6 **Calories:** 164
Exchanges: 2 starch/bread; 1 lean meat

Zucchini Soup

Serves: 4
Cooking time: 8 to 10 minutes
Preparation time: 15 minutes

2 cups Chicken Broth (see index)
2 cups zucchini, sliced
1 cup onion, chopped
3 cloves garlic, smashed
3 dashes dried marjoram
⅛ teaspoon cayenne pepper
  Few dashes celery seed
1 teaspoon curry powder
1 tablespoon tarragon vinegar
  Salt and pepper to taste
2 tablespoons non-fat dry milk
1 cup non-fat yogurt
2 tablespoons diced pimento for garnish (optional)

Place all ingredients except last three in an 8-cup measure, and microwave on High for 8 to 10 minutes until vegetables are tender. Let cool, then puree a little at a time in a food processor or blender. Add milk and yogurt and blend. Chill before serving and garnish with pimento.

Per Serving: 3 Chol (mg) 13 Carbo (g); 5 Prot (g); 91 Na (mg)
Dietary Fiber: 2.6g **Fat (g):** 0; Sat 0; Poly 0; Mono 0 **Calories:** 70
Exchanges: 1 vegetable; ½ skim milk

Fish

Out of the deep blue sea comes a source of protein that is one of the staples of a good nutrition plan. Fish is low in fat and provides essential Omega-3 oils. It is easily prepared, and the microwave proves to be an unbeatable cooking method. Fish cooked in the microwave oven, whether sauced or simply poached, retain their moisture and taste.

Only a few minutes are needed to turn out a tasty and healthful dish.

Hints for Healthy Fish Preparation

▲ Buy only fresh-smelling fish. If it smells fishy, pass it by.

▲ Flesh must be firm and moist and eyes clear. Skin should look shiny but not feel slimy.

▲ Frozen fish retains nutrients but should not smell, contain slushy liquid, or have freezer burn.

▲ Fish should be kept refrigerated or frozen, and it should be consumed within two days of purchase (or thawing).

▲ Fish is cooked when flesh has turned from translucent to opaque and springs back to the touch. Test fish for doneness in its thickest part by cutting into it. If it flakes when pierced with a fork, it is cooked through.

▲ Shrimp are cooked when they turn pink. Do not overcook.

▲ When arranging fish in microwave-safe baking dishes, place thicker edges toward outside and rotate dish during cooking cycle.

▲ Simple fish preparation might include marinating fillets with wine or lemon juice and adding spices such as basil and dill. A little dusting of paprika and pepper and some chopped fresh parsley add color to white fish.

Bluefish Florentine

Serves: 4
Cooking time: 7 to 8 minutes
Preparation time: 15 minutes

- 1 medium onion, sliced
- 1 teaspoon olive oil
- 4 cups spinach leaves, rinsed well, stems trimmed (or 10 ounces frozen spinach, thawed)
- 1 tablespoon frozen orange juice concentrate
- 1 teaspoon olive oil
- 1 teaspoon reduced-sodium soy sauce
- 1 pound bluefish fillets
  Dash paprika
  Dash pepper
- 4 thin slices lemon
  Parsley, chopped, for garnish

Arrange sliced onion and olive oil on microwave-safe platter. Cover with plastic wrap and microwave on High for 2 minutes until onion is tender. Add spinach, cover, and microwave another 2 minutes on High. Let rest covered.

Meanwhile, mix together orange juice, oil, and soy sauce and drizzle over spinach. Set aside and keep warm.

Rinse fish and place in 8 x 10-inch microwave-safe baking dish. Season with paprika and pepper and cover with wax paper. Microwave on High for 3 to 4 minutes, turning once, and rotating dish.

Fish is done when it flakes easily with a fork. Remove fish and place over spinach. Top each fillet with lemon slice and parsley garnish.

Per Serving: 50 Chol (mg); 6 Carbo (g); 19 Prot (g); 142 Na (mg)
Dietary Fiber: 2g **Fat (g):** 6; Sat 1.1; Poly 1.1; Mono 3.0 **Calories:** 154
Exchanges: 1 vegetable; 3 lean meat

Chili Snapper

Serves: 4
Cooking time: 6 minutes
Preparation time: 2 minutes

>   1 pound red snapper fillets
>   Juice of ½ lemon or 1 lime
>   8 ounces Saucy Salsa (see index under "Salsa")

Rinse fish with cold water and arrange, skin-down, on serving platter or in baking dish. Drizzle with lemon or lime juice. Spread salsa over fish and cover with wax paper. Microwave on High for 3 minutes. Remove paper, turn dish, and microwave another 3 minutes until fish flakes easily with fork.

Per Serving: 44 Chol (mg); 7 Carbo (g); 25 Prot (g); 202 Na (mg)
Dietary Fiber: 1.0g **Fat (g):** 2; Sat .3; Poly .5; Mono .3 **Calories:** 141
Exchanges: 3 lean meat; 1 vegetable

Creamy Crabmeat

Serves: 4
Cooking time: 4 to 5 minutes
Preparation time: 15 minutes

> 1 tablespoon pine nuts (pignoli)
> ½ cup part-skim ricotta cheese
> ½ cup low-fat cottage cheese
> 8 ounces lump crab meat (fresh, frozen, or canned), drained and flaked
> 2 tablespoons scallions, chopped
> 2 teaspoons fresh lemon juice
> 1 teaspoon horseradish
> Few dashes cayenne pepper
> Parsley sprigs
> Optional: sliced radishes, carrots, cucumbers, lettuce

Arrange pignoli on a pie plate, and microwave on High for 2 minutes. Chop coarsely and set aside. Blend together the ricotta and cottage cheese. Mix with all remaining ingredients except parsley and optional vegetables.

In a 4-cup glass measure or baking dish, microwave mixture on Medium High (70%) for 2 to 3 minutes until warmed through, stirring once. Top with the chopped pine nuts and parsley sprigs as garnish. This is a nice first course or luncheon dish, served with the optional sliced vegetables on a bed of lettuce.

Per Serving: 61 Chol (mg); 3 Carbo (g); 19 Prot (g); 320 Na (mg)
Dietary Fiber: 0 **Fat (g):** 5; Sat 1.9; Poly .9; Mono 1.3 **Calories:** 128
Exchanges: 3 lean meat

Creole Shrimp

Serves: 4
Cooking time: 7 to 11 minutes
Preparation time: 25 minutes

- 1 16-ounce can Italian plum tomatoes
- 1 medium onion, chopped
- 1 medium green pepper, diced
- ½ teaspoon chili powder
-    Few hot red pepper flakes
- 1 bay leaf
- 1 pound medium-size fresh shrimp, peeled, de-veined, rinsed

In a 2-quart measure or casserole, mix together all ingredients except the shrimp, breaking up tomatoes with a fork. Cover with vented plastic wrap, and microwave on High for 5 to 8 minutes, until green pepper is soft and sauce is bubbling, stirring once.

Add shrimp, stir to mix, cover, and microwave on High for 2 to 3 minutes more until shrimp are pink. Do not overcook. Remove bay leaf, let stand for 3 minutes, and serve over rice if desired.

Per Serving: 174 Chol (mg); 10 Carbo (g); 25 Prot (g); 364 Na (mg)
Dietary Fiber: 2.4g **Fat (g):** 3; Sat .4; Poly 1.0; Mono .3 **Calories:** 160
Exchanges: 3 lean meat; 2 vegetable

Fillets aux Champignons

Serves: 4
Cooking time: 5 to 7 minutes
Preparation time: 15 minutes

> 1 pound scrod fillets (or other thick, white fish such as cod, orange roughy, or pollock)
> 2 tablespoons white wine
> ½ teaspoon dried dill weed
> Few dashes paprika
> 1 cup mushrooms, sliced
> Juice of 1 lemon
> 2 scallions, sliced
> 1 tablespoon fresh basil, chopped, or 1 teaspoon dried basil
> Salt and pepper to taste
> 2 tablespoons toasted pine nuts (pignoli)

Slice the fish into equal portions, wash, and pat dry. Arrange in glass baking dish large enough to hold fillets, with thick sides to the outside. Spoon wine over fish and dust with dill and paprika.

Mix the mushrooms with lemon juice and scallions and spoon over fish, topping with basil. Cover with wax paper and microwave on High 3 to 4 minutes. Rotate dish and microwave on High for another 2 to 3 minutes, until fish is opaque. Season with salt and pepper and garnish with toasted pine nuts.

Per Serving: 24 Chol (mg); 3 Carbo (g); 19 Prot (g); 77 Na (mg)
Dietary Fiber: .6g **Fat (g):** 11; Sat .6; Poly 1.2; Mono 4.8 **Calories:** 184
Exchanges: 3 lean meat

Fillet of Sole Dijonnaise

Serves: 4
Cooking time: 4 to 5 minutes
Preparation time: 15 minutes

1½ pounds fillet of sole
6 medium stalks asparagus, cut diagonally into 2-inch pieces
1 tablespoon low-fat mayonnaise
1½ tablespoons Dijon mustard
Juice of 1 lemon
1 tablespoon chopped chives (dried or frozen fresh)
Dash pepper
Few dashes paprika
Parsley, chopped, for garnish

Arrange fillets in 2-quart baking dish, tucking under thin edges, with thick parts to outside of dish. Arrange asparagus around outside of dish, with one or two stalks in-between fillets.

Mix mayonnaise, mustard, lemon, and chives and spread over fish. Sprinkle with dashes of pepper and paprika.

Microwave on High for 3 to 4 minutes, rotating and moving fillets to cook them evenly. Cover and microwave another 1 minute, until fish flakes easily with a fork. Let stand covered for another minute or two. Top fish with dusting of parsley.

Per Serving: 87 Chol (mg); 3 Carbo, (g); 28 Prot (g); 165 Na (mg)
Dietary Fiber: 1.0 g **Fat (g):** 10; Sat 1.5; Poly 3.8; Mono 3.2 **Calories:** 216
Exchanges: 4 meat

Ginger Shrimp

Serves 4
Preparation time: 25 minutes
Cooking time: 5 minutes

2–3 teaspoons olive oil
1 pound shrimp peeled and deveined (if frozen, defrost)
1 tablespoon fresh ginger, grated
2 tablespoons finely chopped scallions
1 tablespoon chopped red or green bell pepper
1 tablespoon dry vermouth or white wine
2 tablespoons catsup
 dash red pepper flakes

In a shallow 2-quart baking dish combine first five ingredients, arranging shrimp in a circle. Cover with plastic wrap and microwave for 2 to 3 minutes on high power. Add remaining ingredients, stir, cover, and cook for another 1 to 2 minutes or until shrimp are pink. Serve with a green salad and bread or rice.

Per Serving: 140 Chol (mg); 3.5 Carbo (g); 19 Prot (g); 226 Na (mg)
Dietary Fiber: .2g **Fat (g):** 3.9; Sat .6; Poly .8; Mono 1.9 **Calories:** 132
Exchanges: 2½ meat

Gingered Sole

Serves: 4
Cooking time: 3 to 4 minutes
Preparation time: 25 minutes, including marinade resting time

          2 teaspoons low-sodium soy sauce
          1 tablespoon frozen orange juice concentrate
          1 clove garlic, minced
          1 tablespoon sesame oil
          2 teaspoons fresh ginger, minced
      1½ pounds fillet of sole or flounder
            Dash pepper
          1 teaspoon sesame seeds, toasted
            Parsley, chopped, for garnish

In a small jar, mix together soy, orange juice, garlic, sesame oil, and ginger. Shake to blend and let rest at least 15 minutes to develop taste.

In an 8 x 10-inch microwave-safe dish arrange fish, tucking under any thin edges. Spoon sauce over fish and cover with wax paper. Microwave on High for 1½ to 2 minutes. Rotate dish and turn fish. Microwave on High for another 1½ to 2 minutes. Let stand a minute before uncovering, then top fish with dash of pepper, sprinkling of toasted sesame seeds, and chopped parsley.

Per Serving: 85 Chol (mg); 2.1 Carbo (g); 27 Prot (g); 160 Na (mg)
Dietary Fiber: .1g **Fat (g):** 12; Sat 1.8; Poly 4.6; Mono 4.5 **Calories:** 232
Exchanges: 4 lean meat

Grilled Swordfish

Serves: 4
Cooking time: 3 to 4 minutes plus preheating time
Preparation time: 5 minutes

>   1 pound fresh swordfish, about 1-inch thick
>   Few dashes paprika
>   Few dashes dried dill weed
>   4 slices lemon
>   4 small sprigs parsley for garnish

Cut swordfish into 4 steaks. Dust with a little paprika and dill weed. Preheat a 10-inch microwave-safe browning dish on High for 5 minutes. Place steaks on dish, and microwave on High for 1 to 2 minutes.

Drain off excess liquid, turn fish over, and microwave for another 2 minutes on High until fish is no longer pink. Garnish each steak with a lemon slice topped with a parsley sprig. This is a good way to cook tuna steaks, too.

Per Serving: 44 Chol (mg); 1 Carbo (g); 23 Prot (g); 102 Na (mg)
Dietary Fiber: 0 **Fat (g):** 4; Sat 1.2; Poly 1.0; Mono 1.6 **Calories:** 138
Exchanges: 3 lean meat

Hot Garlic Shrimp

Serves: 4
Cooking time: 4 to 5 minutes
Preparation time: 20 minutes

- 1 pound large shrimp
- 1 tablespoon olive oil
- 4 cloves garlic, smashed, peeled, or minced
- ½ to 1 teaspoon red pepper flakes
  - Dash cumin
- 3 tablespoons lemon juice
  - Parsley, chopped, for garnish

Peel and devein shrimp and rinse in cold water. Mix olive oil and garlic in glass measuring cup, and microwave on High for 1 minute.

In a 2-quart round casserole, mix shrimp with oil and garlic, and sprinkle with red pepper, a few dashes of cumin, and lemon juice. Stir to mix, and arrange shrimp in circular fashion, thick ends to the outside of bowl.

Cover with vented plastic wrap, and microwave on High for 3 to 4 minutes, turning shrimp once. Remove when shrimp are pink. Let stand another minute to complete cooking. Dust with parsley.

Per Serving: 174 Chol (mg); 3 Carbo (g); 24 Prot (g); 171 Na (mg)
Dietary Fiber: 0 **Fat (g):** 5; Sat .8; Poly 1.1; Mono 2.8 **Calories:** 156
Exchanges: 3 lean meat

Lemon Trout

Serves: 4
Cooking time: 4 to 7 minutes
Preparation time: 10 minutes

1 pound trout fillets, cut into 4 pieces
4 slices lemon
¼ cup dry white wine
¼ cup shallots, chopped
1 teaspoon lemon peel, grated
½ teaspoon pepper
1 tablespoon parsley, chopped
Dash cayenne

Wash fish and pat dry. Arrange with thick sides outward in an 8 x 12-inch baking dish. Top with lemon slices. Combine wine, shallots, lemon peel, pepper, and parsley and spoon mixture over fish.

Cover with wax paper, and microwave on High for 2 to 3½ minutes. Rearrange fish pieces for even cooking or rotate dish. Microwave, covered, for another 2 to 3½ minutes, until fish flakes easily with a fork. Dust with a little cayenne.

Per Serving: 62 Chol (mg); 2 Carbo (g); 23 Prot (g); 33 Na (mg)
Dietary Fiber: 0.3g **Fat (g):** 4; Sat .7; Poly 1.3; Mono 1.1 **Calories:** 148
Exchanges: 3 lean meat

Lemon Halibut

Serves: 4
Cooking time: 2 minutes
Preparation time: 5 minutes

1½ pounds halibut or haddock fillets

Juice of 2 lemons

Dash of dill weed

Paprika

Pepper

Parsley sprigs for garnish

Rinse and pat dry fish, and arrange in a 2-quart oblong glass baking dish. Spoon lemon juice over fish and dust fillets with dill weed, paprika, and pepper. Cover with vented plastic wrap, and microwave on High for 2 minutes. Fish is done if it flakes easily when pierced with fork. Garnish with a few parsley sprigs.

(Any fish fillets will taste good cooked this simple way. Try it with sole, cod, snapper, or flounder.)

Per Serving: 45 Chol (mg); 3 Carbo (g); 30 Prot (g); 83 Na (mg)
Dietary Fiber: 0 **Fat (g):** 4; Sat .5; Poly 1.2; Mono 1.0 **Calories:** 163
Exchanges: 4 lean meat

Halibut Steaks Marengo

Serves: 4
Cooking time: 8 to 9 minutes
Preparation time: 10 minutes

1½ pounds halibut steaks
Dash salt and pepper
1 medium tomato, diced
¼ cup fresh mushrooms, sliced
1¼ cup onion, sliced
¼ cup celery, diced
1 tablespoon lemon juice
1 tablespoon canola oil
½ teaspoon dried thyme
Parsley, chopped, for garnish

Place fish in shallow baking dish and sprinkle with salt and pepper. Top with diced tomato and set aside.

In a 2-cup measure, mix mushrooms, onion, celery, lemon juice, oil, and thyme. Cover with vented plastic wrap, and microwave on High for 2 to 3 minutes. Spoon over fish.

Microwave fish, covered with wax paper, for 6 minutes on High. Halibut is cooked if it flakes easily when pierced with a fork. Garnish with fresh parsley.

Per Serving: 46 Chol (mg); 6 Carbo (g); 31 Prot (g); 117 Na (mg)
Dietary Fiber: 2.1g **Fat (g):** 7; Sat .8; Poly 1.1; Mono 3.4 **Calories:** 214
Exchanges: 4 lean meat; 1 vegetable

Nutty Sea Scallops

Serves: 4
Cooking time: 6 to 7 minutes
Preparation time: 20 minutes plus marinating time

1¼ pounds sea scallops, halved horizontally
½ cup dry white wine
1 small jalapeno pepper, finely chopped
1 teaspoon olive oil
2 cloves garlic, smashed, peeled, or minced
¼ cup shallots, chopped
Juice of ½ lemon
½ cup green peas (if frozen, thawed)
¼ cup red bell pepper, chopped
1 cup mushrooms, sliced
½ teaspoon dill weed
2 tablespoons peanuts, chopped
Parsley, chopped, for garnish

Marinate scallops in wine with jalapeno pepper for a few hours before cooking.

In an 8 x 12-inch microwave-safe dish, combine oil, garlic, and shallots, and microwave on High for 2 minutes. Add lemon juice, peas, bell pepper, mushrooms, and dill and mix well. Microwave for 2 minutes on High and stir.

Arrange scallops over cooked ingredients, and microwave on High for 2 to 3 minutes, rotating dish once. Let stand a minute before sprinkling on chopped peanuts and dusting of parsley.

Per Serving: 60 Chol (mg); 7 Carbo (g); 29 Prot (g); 342 Na (mg)
Dietary Fiber: 2.2g **Fat (g):** 4; Sat .8; Poly .8; Mono 1.6 **Calories:** 200
Exchanges: 4 lean meat; 1 vegetable

Poached Fish

Serves: 4
Cooking time: 10 minutes
Preparation time: 8 minutes

- 1½ pounds orange roughy fillets, or other white fish such as haddock, cod, pollock
- ½ cup dry white wine
- Pinch salt
- ½ teaspoon white pepper
- ½ teaspoon dried dill
- Dash of paprika
- Sprinkle of celery seed
- 2 tablespoons lemon juice
- 4 lemon slices for garnish
- Parsley, chopped

Place fish fillets in an 8 x 8-inch glass baking dish. Pour wine over fillets and dust with spices and lemon juice. Cover with vented plastic wrap and microwave on Medium (50%) for 10 minutes, rotating dish twice. Let stand covered for another 2 to 3 minutes. Serve warm or chilled with lemon slices, parsley garnish, or a sauce of your choice.

Per Serving: 24 Chol (mg); 1 Carbo, (g); 17 Prot (g); 102 Na (mg)
Dietary Fiber: 0 **Fat (g):** 8; Sat .2; Poly .1; Mono 3.9 **Calories:** 165
Exchanges: 3 lean meat

Salmon Tarragon

Serves: 4
Cooking time: 5 to 6 minutes
Preparation time: 10 minutes

- 1 pound salmon fillet, cut into 4 pieces
- ¼ cup fresh lemon juice
- ½ teaspoon dried tarragon
- Pepper
- 1 tablespoon pimentos, drained, chopped

Wash and pat dry fish fillets. Mix lemon juice, tarragon, and a few dashes of pepper. Arrange fish in a glass baking dish, thick sides outward, and spoon marinade over fillets. Let rest a few minutes to absorb flavor.

Cover with wax paper and microwave on Medium High (70%) for 5 to 6 minutes, until fish flakes easily when pierced with fork. Turn pieces mid-cycle for even cooking. Garnish with pimentos.

Per Serving: 75 Chol (mg); 2 Carbo (g); 24 Prot (g); 60 Na (mg)
Dietary Fiber: 0 **Fat (g):** 9; Sat 1.7; Poly 2.1; Mono 4.5 **Calories:** 188
Exchanges: 3 lean meat

Sole Almondine

Serves: 2
Preparation time: 5 minutes
Cooking time: 4 minutes

1–2 tablespoons butter
2–4 tablespoons slivered blanched almonds
2 tablespoons chopped parsley
2 tablespoons dry white wine
¼ cup chicken broth (see index, or use canned broth)
2 sole fillets (or flounder) about 6 ounces each

Heat 1 tablespoon of butter on high in an 8-inch square browning pan a few seconds. Add almonds and parsley and stir to blend. Cook on high for one minute. Remove dish from oven, add wine and chicken broth, and place fish in center of dish. Cover with plastic wrap and microwave on high for 2½ minutes. Uncover and place on serving dish, whisking remaining butter into almond sauce. Serve with asparagus and light grain.

Per Serving: 51.5 Chol (mg); 2.1 Carbo (g); 15 Prot (g); 221 Na (mg)
Dietary Fiber: 1.1g **Fat (g):** 11.3; Sat 4.3; Poly 1.5; Mono 4.8 **Calories:** 179
Exchanges: 2 meat; 1 fat

Teriyaki Sea Scallops

Serves: 4
Cooking time: 4 to 6 minutes
Preparation time: 10 minutes plus marinating time

2 tablespoons dry sherry

1 tablespoon low-sodium soy sauce

2 tablespoons water

1 tablespoon sesame oil

2 teaspoons ginger root, freshly grated

1 teaspoon frozen orange juice concentrate

2 cloves garlic, minced

1 pound sea scallops

1 tablespoon lemon juice

Paprika

Parsley, chopped, for garnish

Combine sherry, soy sauce, water, oil, ginger, orange juice, and garlic in 8 x 10-inch glass baking dish. Add scallops and marinate in refrigerator up to four hours, turning to coat, or at room temperature for one-half hour.

When ready to cook, cover with vented plastic wrap, and microwave on High for 2 to 3 minutes. Turn scallops over and rotate dish; microwave on High another 2 to 3 minutes. Scallops are cooked when they turn opaque. Let sit, covered, for 3 minutes. Spoon lemon juice over scallops, dust with paprika, and sprinkle on fresh parsley.

Per Serving: 45 Chol (mg); 2 Carbo (g); 20 Prot (g); 380 Na (mg)
Dietary Fiber: 0 **Fat (g):** 5; Sat 1; Poly 1.7; Mono 1.8 **Calories:** 137
Exchanges: 3 lean meat

Tomato/Basil Swordfish Steaks

Serves: 2
Preparation time: 10 minutes
Cooking time: 6–7 minutes

> 1 large ripe tomato, sliced
> 4 leaves fresh basil (or 1 teaspoon dried)
> 8 ounces swordfish steak, about 1 inch thick
> ½ teaspoon olive oil
> 1 teaspoon lemon juice
>   Pinch of salt and black pepper

Arrange tomato slices and half of basil on a microwave-safe platter and top with swordfish. Add next four ingredients and remaining basil. Cover with plastic wrap and microwave on high 4½ minutes. Remove from oven and pierce plastic wrap, then let stand for 2 minutes. Serve with bulgur or couscous and a green vegetable.

Per Serving: 31 Chol (mg); 3.1 Carbo (g); 17 Prot (g); 79 Na (mg)
Dietary Fiber: .7g **Fat (g):** 4.4; Sat 1.0; Poly .9; Mono 2.1 **Calories:** 121
Exchanges: 2 meat

Meat

Beef has been banned from many dietary regimens because of its contribution to high cholesterol. But every so often I yearn to sink my teeth into something other than fish, chicken, or tofu. So a few of my favorite meat recipes are included here for others who are infrequently tempted to "bite the beef." In each case, low fat cuts of meat, well trimmed, have been chosen, and the portions are reasonable. Eaten in moderation, a meat treat will provide additional nutrients.

Attila's Beef Goulash

Serves: 4
Cooking time: 44 minutes plus preheating time
Preparation time: 25 minutes

- 1 pound boneless lean beef chuck, trimmed of all fat, cut into 1-inch cubes
- 3 medium onions, chopped
- 1 large green bell pepper, chopped (about 2 cups)
- 3 cloves garlic, minced
- 1 teaspoon olive oil
- 2 tablespoons Hungarian paprika
- ½ teaspoon salt
- ½ teaspoon black pepper
- 1 tablespoon balsamic vinegar
- 1 cup tomato sauce
- 1 cup fresh mushrooms, sliced

Heat browning dish for 5 minutes on High. When ready, remove from oven and place beef cubes on dish, turning as they brown. Microwave on High for 4 minutes, stirring once. Drain.

Place onions, green pepper, garlic, and oil in a 2-quart measure and microwave on High 5 minutes, stirring once or twice. Meanwhile, combine paprika, salt, and pepper and stir into meat. Add vinegar and tomato sauce.

When vegetables are soft, turn meat mixture into measuring cup and stir to blend. Cover with vented plastic wrap, and microwave on High for 5 minutes. Stir and return to oven. Microwave on Medium (50%) for 30 minutes, stirring a few times. During last 10 minutes, add mushrooms.

Let rest 5 to 10 minutes before serving with noodles, rice, or potatoes. (Goulash is even better if served the following day.)

For a variation, add ¼ cup non-fat plain yogurt if desired.

Per Serving: 90 Chol (mg); 15 Carbo (g); 29 Prot (g); 545 Na (mg)
Dietary Fiber: 4.8 g **Fat (g):** 15; Sat 5.5; Poly .8; Mono 6.6 **Calories:** 309
Exchanges: 3 medium-fat meat; 2 vegetable

Beefsteak Tostadas

Serves: 6
Preparation time: 20 minutes
Cooking time: 15 minutes

1 pound ground sirloin
1 large onion, chopped
½ cup chopped celery
1 can tomato sauce (8 ounces)
1 can red kidney beans, drained (16 ounces)
2 teaspoons chili powder
¼ teaspoon salt
¼ teaspoon dried oregano
½ teaspoon black pepper
½ cup grated Jack cheese
½ cup tortilla chips, crushed
1 cup combined fresh avocado slices, olives, hot pepper slices, chopped tomatoes and shredded lettuce
Dollop sour cream

In a 2–3 quart casserole, combine first three ingredients, cover with plastic wrap, and microwave on high for 5 to 9 minutes. Pour off excess liquid and stir in next six ingredients. Cover again and microwave on high 4 to 5 minutes, stirring during cooking time. Remove from oven, sprinkle with cheese and chips, and microwave for 2 to 3 minutes on high. Remove from oven and top with remaining mixture and dollop of sour cream.

Per Serving: 45 Chol (mg); 22 Carbo (g); 21 Prot (g); 752 Na (mg)
Dietary Fiber: 7g **Fat (g):** 8.4; Sat 3.1; Poly .8; Mono 3.5 **Calories:** 240
Exchanges: 1 starch; 2 meat; 1 fat

Creole Pork Chops

Serves: 4
Cooking time: 25 minutes
Preparation time: 25 minutes

> 4 loin pork chops, 1-inch thick (about 1 pound)
> 1 medium onion, chopped
> 1 small green bell pepper, cut into strips
> ½ cup celery, sliced thin on diagonal
> 2 tablespoons parsley, chopped
> 1 teaspoon chopped green chili peppers (canned)
>   Dash salt and pepper
> 2 cloves garlic, minced
> 1 14-ounce can stewed tomatoes, drained

Trim all fat off chops, rinse, and pat dry. Arrange in 12-inch-square glass baking dish, thick parts to the outside. Add onions, pepper, celery, parsley, and chili peppers. Cover with vented plastic wrap, and microwave on Medium High (70%) for 5 minutes. Rotate dish, turn chops over, and microwave for another 5 minutes.

Add remaining ingredients, cover with vented plastic wrap, and microwave on Medium High (70%) for another 15 minutes, until chops are cooked through. Let stand covered for 5 to 10 minutes before serving.

Per Serving: 77 Chol (mg); 12 Carbo (g); 25 Prot (g); 386 Na (mg)
Dietary Fiber: 2.5 g **Fat (g):** 12; Sat 4.2; Poly 1.6; Mono 5.4 **Calories:** 254
Exchanges: 3 medium-fat meat; 2 vegetable

Gingered Indian Lamb

Serves: 4
Cooking time: 8 minutes
Preparation time: 15 minutes plus refrigerating and resting time

- 1 pound lean lamb
- ¼ cup ginger root, finely chopped
- 1 medium onion, coarsely chopped
- 4 cloves garlic, peeled and smashed
- 8 ounces canned Italian plum tomatoes, drained
  Juice of ½ lemon
- ¼ teaspoon turmeric
- ¼ teaspoon celery seed
- ½ teaspoon cumin
- 1 tablespoon curry powder, mild or hot
- ¼ cup non-fat plain yogurt
- 1 cup frozen peas
- ½ cup fresh mushrooms, sliced (optional)

Trim all fat from lamb and cut, against the grain, into 1-inch pieces. Place ginger root, onions, garlic, and tomatoes in 8 x 10-inch glass baking dish, and cover with vented plastic wrap. Microwave on High for 2 minutes. Remove wrap and stir in all remaining ingredients except peas and mushrooms.

Cover and refrigerate a few hours or overnight. Stir from time to time. When ready to prepare for meal, remove from refrigerator and let rest at room temperature about half an hour. Then cover with vented plastic wrap and microwave on High for 5 minutes. Add peas and mushrooms, and microwave another 1 minute until warmed through.

Per Serving: 81 Chol (mg); 13 Carbo (g); 29 Prot (g); 219 Na (mg)
Dietary Fiber: 4.0 g **Fat (g):** 4; Sat 3.4; Poly .7; Mono 4.2 **Calories:** 256
Exchanges: 4 lean meat; 1 starch/bread

Magic Meatballs

Serves: 4
Preparation time: 10 minutes
Cooking time: 10 minutes

- 1 pound ground sirloin
- 1 egg, beaten
- ½ cup whole wheat breadcrumbs, crushed fine
- ½ teaspoon ground black pepper
- ¼ teaspoon Hungarian paprika
- ½ teaspoon garlic powder
- Dash salt
- Dash dried oregano
- 1 tablespoon Worcestershire or steak sauce

Combine all ingredients and shape into 12 meatballs. Arrange meatballs on a 10-inch deep dish and cover with wax paper. Microwave on High for about 10 minutes, rotating once mid-cycle. Serve with rice or pasta. For variety, may also be prepared with salsa.

Per Serving: 108 Chol (mg); 11 Carbo (g); 23 Prot (g); 200 Na (mg)
Dietary Fiber: .5g **Fat (g):** 5.4; Sat 1.7; Poly .5; Mono 2.2 **Calories:** 191
Exchanges: ½ starch; 3 meat

Meat Loaf Marvel

Serves: 4
Cooking time: 6 to 8 minutes
Preparation time: 20 minutes

> 1 pound 90% lean ground beef (preferably round)
> ¼ cup green pepper, chopped
> ¼ cup red pepper, chopped
> ¾ cup onion, chopped
> 3 cloves garlic, minced
> ½ cup whole wheat bread crumbs
> 1 tablespoon reduced-sodium soy sauce
> 1 tablespoon Dijon mustard
> Dash black pepper
> 1 Vlasic baby dill pickle, chopped

Mix all ingredients together and mold into a long, round loaf, about 2 inches deep. Arrange in circle on a 9-inch pie plate or deep casserole. Microwave on High for 3 to 4 minutes. Baste with sauce and drain off excess. After rotating plate, microwave on High another 3 to 4 minutes.

Per Serving: 84 Chol (mg); 15 Carbo (g); 23 Prot (g); 394 Na (mg)
Dietary Fiber: 1.6 g **Fat (g):** 21; Sat 9.6; Poly 1.2; Mono 9.8 **Calories:** 335
Exchanges: 3 medium-fat meat; 1 starch/bread; 1 fat

Oriental Sliced Beef

Serves: 4
Cooking time: 3 to 5 minutes
Preparation time: 15 minutes

>   2 tablespoons reduced-sodium soy sauce
>   2 tablespoons water
>   1 teaspoon sesame oil
>   1 clove garlic, minced
>   1 teaspoon Dijon mustard
>   1 teaspoon fresh ginger root, grated
>   1 pound lean flank steak, sliced thin across the grain
>   (this is done more easily if steak is partially frozen)
>   1 red bell pepper, julienned
>   4 scallions, chopped
>   1 teaspoon toasted sesame seeds
>   Parsley, chopped, for garnish

Blend first six ingredients and place in a 2-quart casserole. Add sliced meat and stir to coat. Mix in peppers and scallions. Microwave on High 3 to 4 minutes, stirring once. Remove from oven and check for doneness. Some pieces may be more rare than others, and your choice will dictate further cooking for another minute or so. Garnish with sesame seeds and chopped parsley.

Per Serving: 60 Chol (mg); 3 Carbo (g); 23 Prot (g); 389 Na (mg)
Dietary Fiber: 1.0g **Fat (g):** 15; Sat 5.7; Poly 1.1; Mono 6.0 **Calories:** 236
Exchanges: 3 medium-fat meat

Pork and Broccoli Cantonese

Serves: 4
Preparation time: 15 minutes
Cooking time: 15 minutes

⅓ cup water, cold

2 tablespoons low sodium soy sauce

1 tablespoon dry white wine

1 tablespoon cornstarch

1 clove garlic, minced

1 teaspoon grated orange peel

Dash black pepper

3 cups fresh broccoli florets

¾ pound trimmed pork tenderloin, thinly sliced

1 can (8 ounces) sliced water chestnuts, drained

Combine first seven ingredients in a 1½-quart casserole and stir in broccoli. Cover with plastic wrap and microwave on high 4 to 5 minutes, stirring to blend once. Remove from oven and add pork and water chestnuts. Cover again with plastic and microwave on high 9 to 10 minutes. Stir until pork is cooked through. Let stand covered for 2 minutes, then serve over brown rice.

Per Serving: 50 Chol (mg); 14 Carbo (g); 20 Prot (g); 315 Na (mg)
Dietary Fiber: 2.7g **Fat (g):** 2.5; Sat .8; Poly .4; Mono 1.1 **Calories:** 141
Exchanges: 2 veg; 2 meat

Poultry

The great advantage of chicken and turkey is their low cholesterol levels. They also are easy to microwave, but care must be taken that all the pieces are cooked through so that there is no risk of salmonella. For the same reason poultry should never be allowed to sit at room temperature for any length of time. Be sure to wash any utensils and surfaces that come in contact with uncooked poultry. Use a polyurethane cutting board rather than a wooden one, and rinse meat in cold water before cooking.

My preference is boneless and skinless poultry cutlets. However, it may be more economical to buy breasts with the bone in, in which case you will need to remove the skin and cut away the bone. If using a whole chicken, remove the skin by pointing the bird's legs toward you, grasping the skin (using paper toweling), and pulling the skin back from the neck. Cut the skin if necessary and discard.

Poultry combines well with vegetables and a variety of sauces; it may be served alone or with rice, pasta, or potatoes. Poaching boneless chicken or turkey cutlets provides readily cooked morsels for use in a variety of recipes.

To ensure even cooking, slice or cut the poultry into small, evenly sized pieces, and be sure to turn them during the microwaving process. However chicken (or turkey) is prepared, it is a nutritious, low-fat, versatile protein.

Alice's Turkey Enchiladas

Serves: 6
Cooking time: 10 to 15 minutes
Preparation time: 20 minutes

    1   pound lean ground turkey
    ¼   cup onion, chopped
    2   cloves garlic, minced
    8   ounces tomato sauce
    1   teaspoon bottled chilies, chopped
    2   teaspoons chili powder
    1   teaspoon lemon juice
    ½   teaspoon pepper
    ¼   cup green peas (if frozen, thawed)
    4   corn tortillas
    ½   cup shredded part-skim mozzarella or other low-fat
        cheese
        Dash cayenne

Mix ground turkey, onion, and garlic and place in 2-quart casserole. Microwave on High about 4 to 6 minutes, stirring, until turkey loses pink color. Drain.

Stir in tomato sauce, chilies, chili powder, lemon juice, and pepper, and microwave on High for another 4 to 6 minutes, stirring mid-cycle. Stir in peas.

In a 1½-quart baking dish or casserole layer tortillas, turkey mixture, and cheese alternately, topping with some of the cheese and a dash of cayenne. Microwave on High 2 to 3 minutes until cheese bubbles. Let stand a minute or so before serving.

Per Serving: 56 Chol (mg); 14 Carbo (g); 21 Prot (g); 458 Na (mg)
Dietary Fiber: 1.6g **Fat (g):** 15; Sat 5.4; Poly 2.8; Mono 4.5 **Calories:** 272
Exchanges: 1 starch/bread; 3 medium-fat meat

Apricot Turkey Breast

Serves: 4
Cooking time: 5 to 6 minutes
Preparation time: 10 minutes

    1 pound boneless turkey breast
    1 teaspoon paprika
      Pinch cayenne
 1½ tablespoons sugar-free apricot preserve*
    2 teaspoons Dijon mustard
    2 tablespoons parsley, chopped, for garnish

Place turkey breast between two sheets of wax paper and pound with mallet until flattened. Mix paprika and cayenne, and dust one side of turkey with half of mixture. Place, coated side up, on a 10 x 12-inch baking dish. Cover with wax paper and microwave on Medium (50%) for 3 to 4 minutes. Turn, dust with remaining paprika-cayenne mixture, cover, and microwave on Medium another 1 minute until turkey is no longer pink.

Mix apricot preserve with mustard, and coat turkey. Roll up painted turkey and secure with toothpicks. Return to microwave and cook on High another 1 minute. Slice into rounds and serve with garnish of parsley.

*Sugar-free marmalade may be substituted for apricot preserve.

Per Serving: 72 Chol (mg); 1 Carbo (g); 26 Prot (g); 77 Na (mg)
Dietary Fiber: 0 **Fat (g):** 1; Sat .2; Poly .2; Mono .1 **Calories:** 118
Exchanges: 4 lean meat

Chicken Chow Mein

Serves: 4
Cooking time: 11 to 13 minutes
Preparation time: 15 minutes plus 9 minutes poaching time

  1 cup celery, sliced on diagonal
  1 medium green pepper, seeded, cut into thin strips
  1 medium onion, cut into thin wedges
  1 teaspoon canola oil
  1 cup mushrooms, sliced
12 ounces fresh bean sprouts, rinsed and drained
  8 ounces water chestnuts, rinsed and drained
  2 ounces pimentos, drained, chopped
  2 tablespoons reduced-sodium soy sauce
  1 cup Chicken Broth (see index)
  1 tablespoon oat bran
  ¾ pound Poached Chicken (or turkey) Breasts (see index), sliced thinly against grain

In 2-quart glass measure or casserole, combine celery, green pepper, onions, and oil. Microwave on High until tender, about 3 to 4 minutes, stirring once.

Microwave mushrooms for 2 minutes in separate dish and drain when tender. Combine with vegetables, along with bean sprouts, water chestnuts, and pimentos. Mix soy sauce, chicken broth, and oat bran and add to vegetables. Cover with wax paper and microwave on High 5 to 6 minutes, stirring twice.

Add chicken or turkey pieces, mix, and let stand, covered, for 6 or 7 minutes until warmed through. Microwave on High for another minute to heat if necessary. Serve with brown rice and a few chow mein noodles.

Per Serving: 0 Chol (mg); 18 Carbo (g); 32 Prot (g); 401 Na (mg)
Dietary Fiber: 6.6g **Fat (g):** 4; Sat 1.1; Poly .9; Mono 1.8 **Calories:** 238
Exchanges: 3 vegetable; 4 lean meat

Chicken Dijon

Serves: 4
Cooking time: 6 minutes
Preparation time: 10 minutes

1 pound skinless, boneless chicken breast, cut into 4 pieces

2 tablespoons Dijon mustard

2 tablespoons low-fat mayonnaise

Pepper

Paprika

Chives, chopped, for garnish

Place chicken between two pieces of wax paper and pound to thickness of ½ inch. Mix together mustard, mayonnaise, and dashes of pepper and paprika. Coat one side of chicken with half of mustard mixture and place in 8-inch glass baking dish.

Cover with microwave-safe paper towel. Microwave on High for 3 minutes. Turn chicken and coat with remaining mustard sauce. Cover again and microwave on High for another 3 minutes, until chicken is cooked. Garnish with dash of paprika and sprinkling of chopped chives.

Per Serving: 75 Chol (mg); 1 Carbo (g); 27 Prot (g); 202 Na (mg)
Dietary Fiber: 0 **Fat (g):** 6; Sat 1.2; Poly 2.0; Mono 1.7 **Calories:** 169
Exchanges: 4 lean meat

Chicken Livers and Onions

Serves: 4
Preparation time: 10 minutes
Cooking time: 12 minutes

12–16 ounces chicken livers
¼ cup flour
½ teaspoon salt
½ teaspoon black pepper
1 tablespoon olive or canola oil
2 cups thinly sliced onions

Mix together flour, salt, and pepper and toss with livers. Heat oil in a 2-quart casserole for 1 minute on high. Place chicken livers in hot oil and place onions on top of them. Microwave on High for 4 to 5 minutes. Remove from oven, rearrange liver and onions and microwave on Medium (50%) for 5 to 6 minutes.

Per Serving: 373 Chol (mg); 12.7 Carbo (g); 17 Prot (g); 366 Na (mg)
Dietary Fiber: 1.7g **Fat (g):** 6.8; Sat 1.6; Poly .9; Mono 3.3 **Calories:** 181
Exchanges: 1 starch; 2 meat

Chicken Paprikash

Serves: 4
Cooking time: 9 to 10 minutes plus preheating time
Preparation time: 15 minutes

1 pound skinless, boneless chicken breast
1 teaspoon canola oil
2 medium onions, finely chopped
2 cloves garlic, minced
1 medium green pepper, chopped
1 cup mushrooms, sliced
1 cup stewed tomatoes, crushed
2½ to 3 teaspoons sweet Hungarian paprika
1 teaspoon poppy seeds
¼ cup Yogurt Sour Cream (see index)
Salt and pepper to taste

Cut the chicken (against the grain) into thin slices. Heat a browning dish on High for 5 minutes, or follow manufacturer's directions. Brown chicken slices a few at a time and set aside.

Place oil, onions, garlic, and green pepper in a l-quart measure or casserole and microwave on High for 3 minutes, stirring. Add mushrooms and microwave on High another 2 minutes. Mix in tomatoes and paprika, stir to combine, and then add chicken and poppy seeds.

Cover with wax paper and microwave on High for 4 to 5 minutes, stirring once. Remove, let rest a few minutes, then add yogurt sour cream and adjust seasoning. Serve over noodles or rice.

Per Serving: 73 Chol (mg); 13 Carbo (g); 30 Prot (g); 277 Na (mg)
Dietary Fiber: 3.3g **Fat (g):** 5; Sat 1.1; Poly .9; Mono 1.9 **Calories:** 211
Exchanges: 4 lean meat; 2 vegetable

Chicken Salad

Serves: 4
Cooking time: 8 to 10 minutes poaching time
Preparation time: 15 minutes

12 ounces Poached Chicken Breasts (see index)
4 scallions, sliced
3 teaspoons dried basil
1 cup low-fat plain yogurt
2 teaspoons tomato paste
1 teaspoon capers and 1 teaspoon caper juice
Pepper
1 bunch watercress
4 large romaine leaves

Cut chicken diagonally into thin slices or into small chunks. Place in bowl and add scallions and basil. Mix the yogurt, tomato paste, capers, and caper juice and season with pepper.

Trim watercress of tough stems. Chop one-quarter of the bunch and mix it in with the chicken. Combine chicken and yogurt sauce, and serve over romaine leaves. Garnish with remaining watercress.

Per Serving: 73 Chol (mg); 5 Carbo (g); 30 Prot (g); 150 Na (mg)
Dietary Fiber: 2.3g **Fat (g):** 3; Sat 1.0; Poly .7; Mono 1.1 **Calories:** 175
Exchanges: 4 lean meat; 1 vegetable

Chicken Tarragon

Serves: 4
Cooking time: 5 to 7 minutes
Preparation time: 10 minutes plus marinating time

1 pound skinless, boneless chicken breast
2 tablespoons low-sodium soy sauce mixed with
   2 tablespoons water
   Juice of 1 lemon
2 cloves garlic, minced
1 teaspoon sesame oil
2 teaspoons dried tarragon
   Pepper

Trim chicken of any fat and cut into cubes or thin slices. Combine with soy sauce and lemon juice and let marinate 15 minutes.

Place garlic and sesame off in a 1-cup measure and microwave for 1 minute on High. In a l-quart casserole, combine oil and garlic with chicken marinade, add tarragon and pepper, and cover with vented plastic wrap. Microwave on Medium (50%) for 4 to 6 minutes, stirring, until chicken is cooked through.

Per Serving: 72 Chol (mg); 3 Carbo (g); 27 Prot (g); 368 Na (mg)
Dietary Fiber: 0 **Fat (g):** 4; Sat 1.0; Poly 1.2; Mono 1.5 **Calories:** 164
Exchanges: 4 lean meat

Chili con Chicken

Serves: 4
Cooking time: 7 to 9 minutes
Preparation time: 20 minutes

        12 ounces skinless, boneless chicken breasts
         3 tablespoons lemon juice
         1 teaspoon virgin olive oil
         2 cloves garlic, minced
         2 medium onions, sliced
         2 bell peppers (red and green), julienned
         1 teaspoon ground cumin
      1 ½ teaspoons dried oregano
         2 teaspoons fresh chili pepper, finely chopped, or 1 tea-
            spoon dried hot pepper flakes
        ½ teaspoon pepper
         2 tablespoons parsley, chopped, for garnish

Slice chicken into half-inch strips and sprinkle with lemon juice.
Set aside. Place the oil, garlic, and onion in 2-quart casserole, and
microwave on High, uncovered, for 2 minutes. Add pepper strips,
cumin, oregano, and chili pepper. Mix, cover with wax paper, and
microwave on High for another 2 minutes, stirring once. Transfer
to a serving platter.

Top vegetables with chicken strips. Cover with wax paper and
microwave on High for 2 to 3 minutes, then turn chicken pieces.
Microwave on High for another 1 to 2 minutes, until chicken is
no longer pink. Season with pepper and garnish with parsley.

Per Serving: 60 Chol (mg); 6 Carbo (g); 23 Prot (g); 168 Na (mg)
Dietary Fiber: 0 **Fat (g):** 6; Sat 1.2; Poly 1.0; Mono 3.4 **Calories:** 174
Exchanges: 3 lean meat; 1 vegetable

Cantonese Chicken

Serves: 4
Cooking time: 14 to 20 minutes
Preparation time: 20 minutes

- 12 ounces skinless, boneless chicken breasts
- 1 cup broccoli florets
- 1 cup cauliflower florets
- ½ pound mushrooms, sliced
- 4 scallions, cut into 1-inch pieces
- 2 tablespoons low-sodium soy sauce
- 3 tablespoons dry sherry
- 1 teaspoon ginger, freshly grated
- 1 teaspoon arrowroot dissolved in 2 tablespoons water
- 1 teaspoon sesame oil
- ¼ cup unsalted peanuts

Trim all fat off chicken and slice thinly on diagonal. Arrange slices on a flat baking dish, cover with microwave-safe wax paper, and microwave on High for 6 to 8 minutes, turning, until cooked through. Set aside and keep warm, wrapped in foil.

Combine broccoli, cauliflower, mushrooms, scallions, soy sauce, sherry, and ginger in a 2-quart measure. Microwave on High for 6 to 10 minutes, stirring. Add dissolved arrowroot, sesame oil, peanuts, and the chicken pieces. Stir to combine, and microwave on High for 2 minutes until warmed through.

Per Serving: 72 Chol (mg); 9 Carbo (g); 26 Prot (g); 365 Na (mg)
Dietary Fiber: 3.5g **Fat (g):** 9; Sat 1.6; Poly 1.8; Mono 4.4 **Calories:** 223
Exchanges: 3 lean meat; 2 vegetable

Chicken Crunch

Serves: 6
Cooking time: 13 to 16 minutes
Preparation time: 14 to 16 minutes

   1 frying chicken, 2½ to 3 pounds
   1 cup buttermilk
   ½ teaspoon garlic powder
   ½ teaspoon paprika (hot or mild)
   ¼ teaspoon thyme
   ¼ teaspoon salt
   2 cups NutriGrain Cornflakes, finely crushed

Cut chicken into pieces and remove skin with help of paper toweling. Rinse and pat dry. Dip chicken pieces into buttermilk.

Combine all spices and crushed cornflakes in a paper bag. Shake chicken pieces in the bag until coated, and place in 12-inch glass baking dish with thicker pieces toward outside.

Cover with wax paper. Microwave on High for 7 to 8 minutes, then turn chicken pieces and rotate dish. Microwave on High another 6 to 8 minutes.

Per Serving: 102 Chol (mg); 8 Carbo (g); 35 Prot (g); 304 Na (mg)
Dietary Fiber: 0 **Fat (g):** 9; Sat 2.5; Poly 1.9; Mono 3.1 **Calories:** 260
Exchanges: 4 lean meat; ½ starch/bread

Chicken Mexicali

Serves: 4–6
Preparation time: 15 minutes
Cooking time: 22 minutes

16 ounces skinless, boneless chicken breast (4 small breasts)

1 cup chopped onions

1–2 tablespoons olive oil

1 can (16 ounces) stewed tomatoes with liquid

1 small green chili pepper chopped finely

8 ounces baked tortilla chips, crushed

1 cup shredded reduced-fat Cheddar cheese

½ cup pitted black olives, chopped

In a 2-quart casserole, arrange chicken. Cover with plastic wrap and microwave on High 13 minutes or until chicken is done. Cool and slice into small pieces. Set aside, then place onions and olive oil into same casserole and microwave on High for 3 minutes. Add tomatoes, chilies, and chicken pieces and microwave on Medium High (70%) power for 5 to 6 minutes.

Arrange tortilla chips in a medium-size casserole and cover with chicken mixture. Microwave on High for 1 to 2 minutes until hot and top with cheese and olives.

Per Serving: 46 Chol (mg); 65 Carbo (g); 31 Prot (g); 1218 Na (mg)
Dietary Fiber: 7.3g **Fat (g):** 17.8; Sat 4.6; Poly 1.7; Mono 5.2 **Calories:** 619
Exchanges: 3 veg; 3 starch; 2 meat; 2½ fat

Chicken Paillards

Serves: 4
Cooking time: 6 to 7 minutes
Preparation time: 15 minutes

> 1 pound boneless, skinless chicken breasts, halved
> Salt to taste
> ½ teaspoon black pepper
> 1 teaspoon whipped butter
> 1 teaspoon canola oil
> ¼ cup Chicken Broth (see index)
> 2 cloves garlic, minced
> 2 tablespoons fresh lemon juice
> 4 slices lemon
> Paprika
> 2 tablespoons parsley, chopped, for garnish

Place chicken between two sheets of wax paper and pound to half-inch thick paillards. Season each side of chicken with salt and pepper, and set aside in baking dish.

Place butter and oil in a 1-cup glass measure, and microwave on Medium (50%) for 1 minute, until butter melts. Combine with chicken broth, garlic, and lemon juice. Spoon juice over chicken, cover with wax paper, and microwave on High for 5 to 6 minutes, turning once and rotating dish.

Chicken is done when it is no longer pink. Top each paillard with a lemon slice, a dash of paprika and parsley garnish, and spoon sauce over each piece.

Per Serving: 76 Chol (mg); 1 Carbo (g); 26 Prot (g); 135 Na (mg)
Dietary Fiber: 0 **Fat (g):** 7; Sat 2.1; Poly 2.2; Mono 2.1 **Calories:** 189
Exchanges: 4 lean meat

Poached Chicken Breasts

Serves: 4
Cooking time: 8 to 10 minutes
Preparation time: 5 minutes

> 1 pound boneless, skinless chicken breasts
> 1 lemon, sliced thinly
>   Few sprigs parsley

Trim fat from cutlets. Pound to even thickness of about one-half inch between two pieces of wax paper. Arrange in 2-quart glass baking dish, with thicker sides to outside. Add lemon and parsley.

Cover with vented plastic wrap, and microwave on High for 4 to 5 minutes. Flip cutlets over and microwave on High for another 4 to 5 minutes. Poultry is cooked when juices run clear when pricked with a fork. (One pound of boneless chicken breast yields 2 cups of cut-up cooked chicken.)

Turkey cutlets may be prepared in the same way, although the time will be a little less. Poaching a pound of turkey cutlets should take 5 to 8 minutes on High.

Per Serving: 72 Chol (mg); 1 Carbo (g); 27 Prot (g); 67 Na (mg)
Dietary Fiber: 0 **Fat (g):** 3; Sat .9; Poly .7; Mono 1.0 **Calories:** 145
Exchanges: 4 lean meat

Pollo Cacciatore

Serves: 4
Cooking Time: 15 minutes
Preparation Time: 15 minutes

1 can (16 ounces) stewed tomatoes
1 green pepper, chopped coarsely
1 medium onion, chopped
3 cloves garlic, peeled and minced
2 cups sliced fresh mushrooms
1 tablespoon chopped parsley
1 teaspoon dried basil
½ teaspoon dried thyme
   Dash salt
¼ teaspoon black pepper
1 pound chicken cutlets, cut into bite size pieces

Combine all ingredients except chicken in a shallow 2-quart casserole and stir. Cover with plastic wrap and microwave for 5 minutes on High. Uncover, add chicken, re-cover and microwave on Medium High (70%) power for 10 minutes or until chicken is cooked through. Stir and serve over rice or pasta.

Per Serving: 43 Chol (mg); 22 Carbo (g); 21 Prot (g); 568 Na (mg)
Dietary Fiber: 3.7g **Fat (g):** 4.2; Sat .9; Poly 1.3; Mono 1.4 **Calories:** 203
Exchanges: 3 veg; 3 meat

Sesame Chicken

Serves: 4
Cooking time: 6 to 8 minutes
Preparation time: 15 minutes plus marinating time

¼ cup reduced-sodium soy sauce
1 scallion, sliced
1 tablespoon Dijon mustard
1 teaspoon sesame oil
1 tablespoon fresh ginger root, chopped
1 tablespoon frozen orange juice concentrate
1 pound boneless, skinless chicken breast, cut into 1-inch cubes
1 tablespoon toasted sesame seeds
1 tablespoon parsley, chopped, for garnish

Mix together first six ingredients in 1-quart measure. Add chicken and marinate for at least 1 hour, turning a few times. When ready to cook, remove chicken and arrange it in a 9-inch baking dish.

Cover with wax paper and microwave on High for 3 to 4 minutes. Turn chicken pieces, cover again, and microwave on High for another 3 to 4 minutes. Chicken is done when it is white. Sprinkle with sesame seeds and parsley.

Per Serving: 72 Chol (mg); 4 Carbo (g); 28 Prot (g); 711 Na (mg)
Dietary Fiber: 0 **Fat (g):** 5; Sat 1.2; Poly 1.6; Mono 1.9 **Calories:** 180
Exchanges: 4 lean meat

South Indian Chicken Curry

Serves: 4
Cooking time: 9 to 11 minutes
Preparation time: 20 minutes plus marinating time

   2 stalks celery, chopped (about 1 cup)
  ½ cup green pepper, chopped
  ¾ cup fresh mushrooms, chopped
   3 cloves garlic, minced
   1 small onion, chopped
   1 tablespoon fresh ginger root, minced
   1 tablespoon olive oil
  ⅛ teaspoon turmeric
  ¼ teaspoon ground cumin
   1 tablespoon mild curry powder
  ½ cup non-fat plain yogurt
   1 pound skinless, boneless chicken breast, sliced thinly on diagonal

Place first 6 ingredients and oil in 1-quart glass measure and microwave on High for 3 minutes, stirring once. Mix spices with yogurt. Turn all ingredients, including chicken, into a casserole and let marinate for several hours.

Before cooking, bring to room temperature. Cover with lid or paper towels, and microwave on High for 3 to 4 minutes. Stir and return to microwave; cook on High another 3 to 4 minutes. Serve with basmati rice, noodles, or on top of baked potato halves.

Per Serving: 73 Chol (mg); 6 Carbo (g); 29 Prot (g); 113 Na (mg)
Dietary Fiber: 1.9g **Fat (g):** 7; Sat 1.4; Poly 1.0; Mono 3.6 **Calories:** 203
Exchanges: 4 lean meat; 1 vegetable

Turkey Cutlets with Peppers

Serves: 4
Cooking time: 10 minutes
Preparation time: 20 minutes

1–2 tablespoons virgin olive oil
1 large onion sliced
1 red bell pepper, seeded, cut into strips
1 yellow bell pepper, seeded, cut into strips
6 ripe plum tomatoes, quartered
Pinch salt
¼ teaspoon ground black pepper
1 pound turkey breast cutlets, pounded thin, cut into 4 pieces

Heat olive oil for 1 minute, uncovered, in a microwave dish 14 x 11 x 2. Add sliced onions, stir, and microwave on High uncovered for 2 minutes. Remove from oven and add peppers, tomatoes, salt, and pepper. Stir to coat and mound vegetables in center of dish. Place turkey cutlets around vegetables, cover with plastic wrap, and microwave on High for 8 minutes. Remove from oven, let stand 1 minute and check for doneness.

Per Serving: 48 Chol (mg); 16 Carbo (g); 21 Prot (g); 57 Na (mg)
Dietary Fiber: 3.6g **Fat (g):** 5.4; Sat .9; Poly .9; Mono 2.8 **Calories:** 192
Exchanges: 2 veg; 3 meat

Turkey Peppercorn

Serves: 4
Cooking time: 2 to 3 minutes
Preparation time: 10 minutes

> 1 pound turkey breast cutlets, pounded to ¼-inch thickness
>
> 1 tablespoon black (or green) peppercorns, crushed in blender
>
> ½ cup dry white wine
>
> 1 tablespoon brandy
>
> 1 tablespoon parsley, chopped, for garnish

Rinse turkey cutlets and pat dry. Press crushed peppercorns firmly into both sides of turkey cutlets. Smack cutlets with the side of a cleaver or saute pan to make peppercorns adhere. Place cutlets in 12-inch glass casserole, and add wine and brandy. Microwave on High for 2 to 3 minutes. Stir. Serve with garnish of parsley.

Per Serving: 78 Chol (mg); 1 Carbo (g); 25 Prot (g); 68 Na (mg)
Dietary Fiber: 0 **Fat (g):** 1; Sat .2; Poly .2; Mono .1 **Calories:** 158
Exchanges: 4 lean meat

Turkey Marsala

Serves: 4
Cooking time: 4 to 7 minutes plus preheating time
Preparation time: 10 minutes

- 12 ounces turkey breast cutlets, sliced thin on diagonal
- 1 teaspoon dried rosemary, crushed
- 2 tablespoons Marsala (or sherry)
- ¼ cup dry white wine
- Pepper
- Parsley sprigs for garnish

Heat a browning dish on High for 5 minutes in the microwave. Place half of turkey slices on dish, and microwave on High for 1 to 2 minutes. Repeat with remaining turkey slices. Combine turkey slices and microwave on High until no longer pink, about 1 minute.

Mix rosemary and wine and let steep a few minutes. When turkey is white, add wine mixture and microwave another 1 to 2 minutes on High. Season with fresh pepper and serve with parsley garnish. Let stand a few minutes before serving.

Per Serving: 75 Chol (mg); 1 Carbo (g); 26 Prot (g); 57 Na (mg)
Dietary Fiber: 0 **Fat (g):** 1; Sat .2; Poly .2; Mono .1 **Calories:** 135
Exchanges: 3 lean meat

Turkey Teriyaki

Serves: 4
Cooking time: 7 to 10 minutes
Preparation time: 10 minutes plus marinating time

- 1 pound turkey breast or skinless, boneless chicken breasts
- 2 tablespoons low-sodium soy sauce mixed with 2 tablespoons water
- 1 tablespoon Dijon mustard
- 2 tablespoons fresh ginger root, grated
- 2 cloves garlic, minced
- 1 tablespoon orange rind, grated
- 1 teaspoon sesame oil
- ¼ cup dry sherry
- 2 cups mushrooms, sliced
- 1 cup green peas (if frozen, thawed)

Wash the turkey or chicken and pat dry. Cut into half-inch cubes. Blend remaining ingredients, except mushrooms and peas, and pour over turkey. Let turkey marinate for at least 1 hour, or preferably overnight in refrigerator. Turn several times.

Place mushrooms in 1-quart measure, and microwave on High for 2 minutes until soft. Drain and reserve.

Place turkey with some of marinade in 8-inch square baking dish and cover with wax paper. Microwave on High 2 to 3 minutes. Turn poultry pieces and rotate dish. Microwave on High another 2 to 3 minutes.

Add mushrooms and peas, and microwave on High for another 1 to 2 minutes until warmed through. Serve with rice or noodles.

Per Serving: 72 Chol (mg); 9 Carbo (g); 29 Prot (g); 430 Na (mg)
Dietary Fiber: 3.2g **Fat (g):** 2; Sat .4; Poly .8; Mono .6 **Calories:** 183
Exchanges: 4 lean meat; ½ starch/bread

Grains

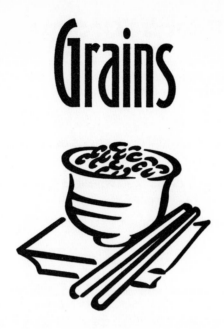

Grains provide many minerals and vitamins and may be prepared in myriad ways. Many of them can be main dishes, with the addition of vegetables, bits of fish or poultry, nuts, or low-fat cheese. Grains are also adaptable as desserts, in addition to their usual use as side dishes.

The microwave makes cooking grains a matter of minutes rather than long, stove-top simmering. A creamy risotto made with arborio rice is now a simple matter, and wild rice (which is actually a grass) and barley become delectable in short order. Try quinoa, an ancient Peruvian grain that has many health-giving qualities. You'll enjoy these complex-carbohydrate recipes as a welcome change from potatoes and pasta.

Bulgur Pilaf à l'Orange

Serves: 6
Cooking time: 24 to 27 minutes
Preparation time: 15 minutes plus standing time

> ¼ cup currants
> 2 tablespoons sunflower seeds or slivered almonds
> Rind and juice of 1 orange
> ¾ cup bulgur or cracked wheat (3 cups cooked)
> 1 teaspoon sesame oil
> 1 small onion, chopped
> 1½ cups water

In a blender, process currants, sunflower seeds, orange rind, and juice. Set aside. Place bulgur, sesame off, and onion in an 8-cup measure, and microwave on High for 2 minutes. Stir.

In another cup, bring water to boil on High (5 to 6 minutes); then add water to bulgur and microwave on High for 5 minutes. Combine with orange mixture, reduce power to Medium (50%), and microwave for 12 to 14 minutes. Let stand until liquid is absorbed. Makes 4 cups.

Per Serving: 0 Chol (mg); 22 Carbo (g); 4 Prot (g); 1 Na (mg)
Dietary Fiber: 1.6g **Fat (g):** 4; Sat .4; Poly 2.1; Mono .8 **Calories:** 131
Exchanges: 1½ starch/bread; 1½ fat

Fluffy Kasha

Serves: 4
Cooking time: 9 to 11 minutes
Preparation time: 5 minutes plus standing time

1½ cups water
2 teaspoons sesame oil
½ cup kasha (buckwheat groats)
1 egg white
2 cloves garlic, smashed
1 teaspoon reduced-sodium soy sauce
2 teaspoons sesame seeds
Pepper to taste

Bring water to boil, microwaving on High for 5 to 6 minutes. In another 2-quart measure, mix the sesame oil and kasha. Microwave for 1 to 2 minutes until toasted. Stir in egg white and microwave on High another 30 seconds.

Add boiling water and simmer on High 2 minutes. Add garlic and soy sauce and microwave on High for another 30 seconds. Let stand for 5 minutes. Add sesame seeds, season with pepper, and fluff with a fork.

Variation: microwave one-half cup each mushrooms, onions, and celery with a teaspoon of sesame oil for 2 minutes until tender, and fluff in when kasha is cooked. Peas, zucchini, and spinach may also be combined with groats.

Per Serving: 0 Chol (mg); 17 Carbo (g); 4 Prot (g); 86 Na (mg)
Dietary Fiber: .6g **Fat (g):** 3; Sat .4; Poly 1.2; Mono 1.2 **Calories:** 109
Exchanges: 1 starch/bread

Golden Barley

Serves: 4
Cooking time: 30 minutes
Preparation time: 5 minutes

> 2 cups water
> ½ cup pearl barley
> 1 tablespoon golden raisins
> 1 tablespoon almonds
> 1 tablespoon peanuts
> ¼ cup celery, chopped
> Pinch ground cardamom
> Salt and pepper to taste

Bring water to boil in 1-quart microwave measure and add barley.
Cook on High for 30 minutes, stirring a few times. When barley
is tender, drain, and stir in remaining ingredients. Serve warm or
chilled as a salad. Dressing may be added as desired.

Per Serving: 0 Chol (mg); 22 Carbo (g); 2 Prot (g); 34 Na (mg)
Dietary Fiber: 3.2g **Fat (g):** 1; Sat .1; Poly .2; Mono .4 **Calories:** 103
Exchanges: 1½ starch/bread; 1 vegetable

Green Pea Risotto

Serves: 6
Cooking time: 16 to 20 minutes
Preparation time: 7 minutes plus standing time

1¾ cups Chicken Broth (see index)
1 tablespoon olive oil
1 tablespoon whipped butter
1 onion, finely chopped
¾ cup arborio rice
2 tablespoons dry white wine
½ cup frozen peas, thawed
2 tablespoons Parmesan or Romano cheese, grated
Salt and pepper to taste

Place broth in a 4-cup measure, and microwave on High for 3 to 4 minutes, until it simmers. Place oil, butter, and onion in 1-quart measure, and microwave on High for 2 minutes, until onions are soft. Add rice and stir to coat.

Pour in hot chicken broth and wine. Cover with vented plastic wrap. Microwave on High for 4 to 5 minutes, until boiling. Microwave on Medium (50%) for 7 to 9 minutes more until rice is tender. Rotate dish, stir in peas, and let stand covered 5 minutes. Stir in cheese and season with salt and pepper.

Per Serving: 4 Chol (mg); 22 Carbo (g); 3 Prot (g); 235 Na (mg)
Dietary Fiber: 1.6g **Fat (g):** 4; Sat 1.3; Poly .3; Mono 2.1 **Calories:** 146
Exchanges: 1½ starch/bread; 1 fat

Jane's Millet Primavera

Serves: 6
Cooking time: 24 to 25 minutes
Preparation time: 20 minutes

¾ cup millet (available in natural food stores)

2 tablespoons olive oil

1 medium onion, chopped

2 stalks celery, diced

1 green or red pepper, diced

1 carrot, diced

1 small zucchini, diced (about ½ cup)

2 cloves garlic, minced

1 teaspoon fresh ginger root, diced

2½ cups Chicken Broth (see index)

1 teaspoon curry powder (or more if desired)

½ teaspoon dried dill weed

Salt and pepper to taste

Spread millet on a 9-inch pie plate, and toast in microwave on High for 1 minute. In a 2-quart casserole or measure combine next eight ingredients, and microwave on High for 3 to 4 minutes.

Add toasted millet and chicken broth, along with curry and dill weed. Cover with vented plastic wrap, and microwave on High for 20 minutes, stirring a few times. When grain is tender, season with salt and pepper to taste. Makes 3 ½ cups.

Per Serving: 0 Chol (mg); 22 Carbo (g); 3 Prot (g); 284 Na (mg)
Dietary Fiber: 2.3g **Fat (g):** 5; Sat .8; Poly .8; Mono 3.9 **Calories:** 130
Exchanges: 1 vegetable; 1 starch/bread; 1 fat

Matzo Meal Polenta

Serves: 6
Cooking time: 6 to 9 minutes
Preparation time: 10 minutes

> 2 cups Chicken Broth (see index)
> Generous pinch turmeric
> ⅔ cup matzo meal
> ½ teaspoon hot red pepper flakes
> Salt and pepper to taste
> 1 cup mushrooms, sliced
> ½ cup onions, sliced
> 1 teaspoon olive oil
> 1 teaspoon Romano cheese, grated
> Tomato sauce (optional)

In a 2-quart measure, microwave broth on High for 3 minutes, until it boils. Add turmeric and stir. Add matzo meal, red pepper flakes, salt, and pepper, and microwave on High for 2 to 4 minutes, stirring once, until all liquid is absorbed. Turn into serving dish.

Place mushrooms and onions in a 2-cup bowl with olive oil, and microwave on High for 1 to 2 minutes, until tender. Top the matzo meal polenta with the vegetables and a dusting of cheese. Tomato sauce may also be used as topping if desired. May be served chilled.

Per Serving: 0 Chol (mg); 10 Carbo (g); 2 Prot (g); 95 Na (mg)
Dietary Fiber: 1.0g **Fat (g):** 1; Sat .2; Poly .5 Mono .3 **Calories:** 54
Exchanges: 1 starch/bread

Pimento Polenta

Serves: 4
Cooking time: 16 to 20 minutes
Preparation time: 10 minutes

2 cups Chicken Broth (see index)
½ cup yellow cornmeal
½ cup corn niblets, drained (fresh, canned, or frozen)
1 tablespoon olive oil
Pinch salt
¼ teaspoon cayenne
½ teaspoon dried thyme
½ teaspoon dried oregano
2 tablespoons Parmesan cheese, grated
Dash pepper
¼ cup pimentos, sliced, for garnish

Place chicken broth in a 2-quart microwave-safe bowl, and microwave on High for 4 to 6 minutes to heat. To the broth, add cornmeal, niblets, olive oil, and next four seasonings. Microwave uncovered on High for 12 to 15 minutes, stirring every 5 minutes. When polenta is tender and liquid is absorbed, stir in Parmesan cheese and pepper. Spoon into serving dish and top with pimentos.

Variations:
1. Slice and serve with topping of salsa or tomato sauce.
2. Add microwaved onions, red or green peppers, and sliced mushrooms.
3. Mix with a little blue cheese, Gorgonzola, or goat cheese.
4. Top with part-skim ricotta and a few cooked green peas or chopped broccoli.

Per Serving: 3 Chol (mg); 21 Carbo (g); 4 Prot (g); 123 Na (mg)
Dietary Fiber: 3.2g **Fat (g):** 5; Sat 1.0; Poly .5; Mono 2.9 **Calories:** 134
Exchanges: 1½ starch/bread; 1 fat

Inca Pilaf

Serves: 4
Cooking time: 24 minutes
Preparation time: 10 minutes

- ¼ cup red bell pepper, diced
- 2 cloves garlic, minced
- 1 small onion, chopped
- 1 teaspoon sesame oil
- ¾ cup quinoa (once eaten by the Incas, it is now available in natural food stores and some supermarkets; pronounced "keen-wa")
- 1½ cups Chicken Broth (see index)
- ½ cup green peas

Place pepper, garlic, onion, and sesame oil in a 4-cup glass measure. Microwave uncovered on High for 2 minutes, and stir. Add quinoa and broth and microwave on High for 5 minutes, stirring once. Microwave on Medium (50%) for 15 minutes. Add peas; stir to mix. Microwave on High another 2 minutes or until liquid is absorbed. Grains should be pearly, with white outline visible. Fluff with a fork.

Per Serving: 0 Chol (mg); 17 Carbo (g); 3 Prot (g); 289 Na (mg)
Dietary Fiber: 2.1g **Fat (g):** 2; Sat .2; Poly .6 Mono .5 **Calories:** 93
Exchanges: 1 starch/bread

Piquant Couscous

Serves: 4
Cooking time: 5 minutes
Preparation time: 5 minutes plus resting time

1 cup orange juice

½ cup water

1 cup Moroccan couscous

½ teaspoon orange zest, grated

⅛ teaspoon ground cardamom

Few dashes ground ginger

1 teaspoon poppy seeds

2 tablespoons non-fat plain yogurt

1 tablespoon pecans, chopped

1 teaspoon coconut, shredded

Combine all ingredients except last three in a 1-quart casserole. Microwave on High for 5 minutes or until all liquid is absorbed, stirring mid-cycle. Let rest 5 minutes before stirring in yogurt. Garnish with pecans and coconut.

Per Serving: 0 Chol (mg); 28 Carbo (g); 5 Prot (g); 17 Na (mg)
Dietary Fiber: .8g **Fat (g):** 1; Sat .2; Poly .1; Mono .4 **Calories:** 142
Exchanges: 2 starch/bread

Wild Rice

Serves: 4
Cooking time: 37 minutes
Preparation time: 10 minutes plus standing time

1	teaspoon canola oil
¼	cup shallots, chopped
½	cup celery, chopped
¾	cup wild rice
2½	cups Chicken Broth (see index)
2	tablespoons pine nuts (pignoli)

Combine oil with shallots and celery in a 2-cup measure, and microwave on High for 2 minutes or until tender. Rinse rice well, discarding any debris that floats to surface. Drain. Place wild rice and chicken broth in 2-quart glass measure. Microwave on High for 5 minutes, then stir. Microwave on Medium (50%) for 30 minutes longer. Let stand for 10 minutes, and drain off any excess liquid. When rice is ready to serve, stir in vegetables and pine nuts.

Variations:
1. Add cooked mushrooms and chopped parsley.
2. Substitute walnuts for pignoli.
3. Add currants and shredded part-skim mozzarella cheese.
4. Use half brown rice, half wild rice.

Per Serving: 0 Chol (mg); 26 Carbo (g); 6 Prot (g); 467 Na (mg)
Dietary Fiber: 2.89 **Fat (g):** 4; Sat .6; Poly 1.2; Mono 1.7 **Calories:** 153
Exchanges: 2 starch/bread; 1 fat

Carbohydrates

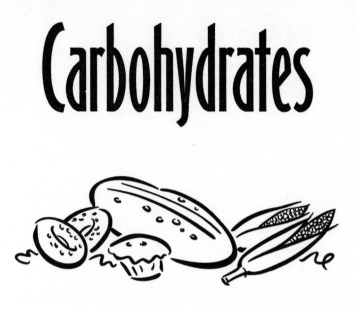

Beans and legumes are a wonderful source of energy. Combined with rice, a whole protein is achieved. Combinations of peppers, onions, other vegetables, and tomato sauces provide color, texture, and taste to the healthful bean, which ranges from white to black, with pink, red, and green in between.

Curried Lentils

Serves: 10 (half-cup servings)
Cooking time: 33 to 38 minutes
Preparation time: 10 minutes

1 tablespoon olive oil

3 shallots, minced (about ⅓ cup)

1 carrot, finely chopped

2 cloves garlic, minced

¾ cup brown (or orange) lentils

3 cups Chicken Broth, as needed (see index)

½ teaspoon fresh ginger root

1 teaspoon curry powder

2 stalks celery, chopped small

Few dashes reduced-sodium soy sauce

Few dashes sesame oil

2 tablespoons non-fat plain yogurt (optional)

In a 2-quart measure or casserole, combine olive oil, shallots, carrot, and garlic. Microwave on High for 3 minutes, stirring once, until tender. Add lentils, broth, and ginger and cover with vented plastic wrap.

Microwave on High for 30 to 35 minutes, stirring a few times. Lentils should be tender but crunchy. Drain off any excess liquid. Stir in curry powder, celery, soy, and sesame oil. Add yogurt to moisten if desired. Makes 5 cups.

Per Serving: 2 Chol (mg); 11 Carbo (g); 4 Prot (g); 230 Na (mg)
Dietary Fiber: 5.8g **Fat (g):** 2; Sat .3; Poly .3; Mono .9 **Calories:** 72
Exchanges: 1 starch/bread

Green and Red Beans

Serves: 4
Cooking time: 6 minutes
Preparation time: 5 minutes

½ cup celery, chopped
2 large scallions, chopped
2 cloves garlic, minced
¼ cup green pepper, chopped
½ teaspoon dried oregano
⅛ teaspoon cayenne
8 ounces kidney or pinto beans (if canned, beans should be rinsed and drained)
1 teaspoon Vogue chicken-flavored base
1 teaspoon sesame seeds

Place celery, scallions, garlic, green pepper, and spices in a 2-cup measure. Microwave on High for 5 minutes. Add beans and chicken flavoring, and microwave 1 minute on High. Stir to mix. When warmed through, toss with sesame seeds. Serve with brown rice if desired.

Per Serving: 0 Chol (mg); 13 Carbo (g); 4 Prot (g); 225 Na (mg)
Dietary Fiber: 3.0g **Fat (g):** 1; Sat .1; Poly .3; Mono .2 **Calories:** 72
Exchanges: 1 starch/bread

Mid-Eastern Kidney Beans

Serves: 4
Cooking time: 7 minutes
Preparation time: 10 minutes

1 medium onion, chopped

1 clove garlic, minced

1 teaspoon olive oil

1 16-ounce can kidney or pinto beans, rinsed and drained

Juice of 1 lemon and ½ teaspoon lemon rind

1 teaspoon dried oregano, crushed

Pepper to taste

Few sprigs parsley for garnish

Lemon wedges for garnish

Place onion, garlic, and oil in a 4-cup measure, and microwave on High for 2 minutes. Add kidney or pinto beans, and microwave on High for 5 minutes. Mix lemon juice, lemon rind, and oregano and pepper to taste. Stir this mixture into beans and mash lightly with a fork. Garnish with parsley sprigs and lemon wedges. Serve as appetizer on bed of greens or as a side dish.

Per Serving: 0 Chol (mg); 24 Carbo (g); 8 Prot (g); 473 Na (mg)
Dietary Fiber: 5.4g **Fat (9):** 2; Sat .2; Poly .4; Mono .8 **Calories:** 133
Exchanges: 1½ starch/bread

Spanish Chick Peas

Serves: 6
Cooking time: 6 minutes
Preparation time: 15 minutes

1 medium onion, finely chopped

2 cloves garlic, minced

2 teaspoons olive oil

1 16-ounce can garbanzos (chick peas), rinsed and drained

1 medium tomato, chopped

2 tablespoons parsley, chopped

3 leaves fresh basil, or ½ teaspoon dried basil
Ground pepper to taste

Mix onion, garlic, and oil in a 2-quart measure, and microwave on High 2 minutes, uncovered. Add remaining ingredients, and microwave on High 4 minutes, stirring once. Serve warm or chilled. May be used as appetizer, salad, or side dish.

Per Serving: 0 Chol (mg); 13 Carbo (g); 4 Prot (g); 259 Na (mg)
Dietary Fiber: 4g **Fat (g):** 3; Sat .2; Poly .2; Mono 1.0 **Calories:** 86
Exchanges: 1 starch/bread

Potatoes

According to Jane Brody, writing in *The New York Times*, "The potato can supply more nutritious food faster than any other foodstuff. With almost no fat, a vegetable protein that is nearly as nourishing as milk protein and a laundry list of vitamins and minerals, the potato comes close to being a perfect source of nourishment."

Potatoes lend themselves to a variety of cooking styles. The microwave bakes potatoes differently from the conventional oven; the skins will not be crisp but it only takes a few minutes. A chart for baking times, depending on the number of potatoes, is given in the recipe for Stuffed Potatoes.

Lyonnaise Potatoes

Serves: 4
Cooking time: 12 to 14 minutes
Preparation time: 15 minutes

2 Idaho potatoes, about 8 ounces each, sliced thin, about ⅛-inch thick

2 medium onions, sliced thin

1 tablespoon olive oil

3 cloves garlic, minced

¼ teaspoon salt

⅛ teaspoon pepper

⅛ teaspoon paprika

1 tablespoon parsley, chopped, for garnish

Place all ingredients, except parsley, in a microwave-safe 3-quart casserole. Cover loosely with plastic wrap, and microwave on High for 12 to 14 minutes, until tender, stirring gently a few times. Garnish with parsley and let stand a few minutes before serving.

Per Serving: 0 Chol (mg); 18 Carbo (g); 3 Prot (g); 118 Na (mg)
Dietary Fiber: .7g **Fat (g):** 4; Sat .5; Poly .4; Mono 2.5 **Calories:** 108
Exchanges: 1 starch/bread; 1 fat

New Potato Salad

Serves: 4
Cooking time: 10 to 12 minutes
Preparation time: 10 minutes

6 new potatoes, well washed
¾ cup celery, chopped (about 3 medium stalks)
¼ cup non-fat plain yogurt
1 tablespoon reduced-calorie mayonnaise
2 tablespoons tarragon vinegar
1 tablespoon Dijon mustard
1 tablespoon fresh lemon juice
1 teaspoon low-sodium soy sauce
1 tablespoon caraway seeds
Romaine or spinach leaves
Tomatoes or other fresh vegetables for garnish

Place potatoes in large glass casserole with a little water. Cover with paper towel. Microwave on High for 10 to 12 minutes, until tender but not too soft, rotating twice. Let cool and cut into quarters.

Meanwhile for dressing, blend together the remaining ingredients except seeds, lettuce, and garnish. Mix potatoes with dressing, toss in caraway seeds, and serve on bed of lettuce or spinach with garnish of fresh vegetables.

Per Serving: 0 Chol (mg); 21 Carbo (g); 3 Prot (g); 155 Na (mg)
Dietary Fiber: 3.2g **Fat (g):** 2; Sat .3; Poly .5; Mono .7 **Calories:** 109
Exchanges: 1 ½ starch/bread

Stuffed Potatoes

Serves: 4
Cooking time: 17 to 21 minutes
Preparation time: 10 minutes

Potatoes

4 small Idaho baking potatoes, well washed but not dried. Pierce each potato once through the skin at the center. Wrap in microwave-safe paper towel, and place end-to-end in a circle on the floor of the oven. Microwave on High for 16 to 20 minutes. If baking fewer than four potatoes, follow this cooking guide:

> One potato (8 ounces): 4 to 5 minutes
>
> Two potatoes: 7 to 10 minutes
>
> Three potatoes: 11 to 14 minutes

When potatoes are cooked, leave in paper for another minute until ready to stuff.

Yogurt Sour Cream Stuffing

> ¼ cup plain Yogurt Sour Cream (see index)
>
> 2 tablespoons Parmesan or Romano cheese, grated
>
> Chives, snipped
>
> Dash paprika

Cut potatoes in half, lengthwise, and scoop out meat. Mix with yogurt sour cream and cheese and stuff back into shells. Top with garnish of chives and dash of paprika. Return to microwave for 1 minute on High to warm through, or, if desired, run under broiler until top browns lightly.

Per Serving: 3 Chol (mg); 22 Carbo (g); 6 Prot (g); 98 Na (mg)
Dietary Fiber: 3.6g **Fat (g):** 1; Sat .6; Poly .1; Mono .2 **Calories:** 116
Exchanges: 1½ starch/bread

Turnip Yam Treat

Serves: 4
Cooking time: 11 to 13 minutes
Preparation time: 20 minutes

2 medium turnips, peeled and cubed
2 medium yams, peeled and cubed
¼ cup water
¼ cup non-fat dry milk
¼ teaspoon nutmeg
  Dash dried thyme
1 tablespoon frozen apple juice concentrate
  Salt and pepper to taste

Place cubed turnips and yams in 2-quart glass measure or casserole with water. Cover with paper towel, and microwave on High for 10 to 12 minutes, stirring twice, until tender.

Turn into blender or food processor, add remaining ingredients, and puree. Return to microwave to warm for 1 minute if necessary. Season with salt and pepper. This is especially attractive if served in the center of a ring of broccoli.

Per Serving: 1 Chol (mg); 27 Carbo (g); 3 Prot (g); 98 Na (mg)
Dietary Fiber: 4.4g **Fat (g):** 0; Sat 0; Poly 0; Mono 0 **Calories:** 116
Exchanges: 2 starch/bread

Pasta

More and more frequently, pasta is becoming the food of choice for health-conscious people. Nutritionally speaking, pasta is an ideal food. It is low in fat and cholesterol and high in complex carbohydrates, protein, B vitamins, and iron. Because it is digested slowly, it is a boon to people with diabetes since it helps maintain an even blood sugar level.

Pasta is easy to cook, versatile, and lends itself to many inventions, from the addition of fresh vegetables, seafood, or chicken to dressing with light mock cream sauces, such as a combination of part-skim ricotta and yogurt, or oriental hot sauces. The creative chef will enjoy making personal pasta dishes for the entire family. It is recommended that pasta be cooked on top of a conventional range and the sauce be cooked in the microwave oven.

Simple Pasta Preparations

Toss hot pasta with a little freshly grated Parmesan or Romano cheese, fresh-minced garlic, and fresh pepper.

Microwave wedges of fresh tomatoes for 1 minute and toss over pasta with fresh-minced basil and a tablespoon of olive oil.

Rinse a can of kidney or pinto beans and heat in the microwave with a few finely chopped walnuts and a tablespoon of olive or peanut oil. Add a dash of pepper for taste.

Popular Pasta Shapes

More than 150 different pasta shapes are made in the United States, and there are even more imported from Italy. It is also possible to purchase freshly made, flavored pastas in specialty food shops. Some of these are flavored with seafood, Cajun spices, or vegetables such as tomatoes and spinach. These are some of the more readily available and popular shapes:

Capellini, or Angel Hair
Conchiglie—shells: small, medium and large
Ditalini—small macaroni
Egg noodles
Elbow macaroni
Farfalle—bow ties
Fettucine—small ribbons
Fettucine verde—spinach ribbons
Fusilli—twisted spaghetti
Linguine—flat spaghetti
Orzo—small quill-shaped pasta
Penne—large quill-shaped pasta
Rigatoni—ribbed large quills
Rotelle—spiral-shaped pasta
Rotini—twists, often available in tri-color tastes
Ruote—wheels
Spaghetti
Vermicelli—thin spaghetti strands
Ziti—large tubes, sometimes called "bridegrooms"

Wheat-free pasta made of Jerusalem artichokes is also available and is flavorful as well as safer for those who may have wheat allergies. Spinach-flavored pasta is made by DeBoles, the same manufacturer of the wheat-free spaghetti. Buckwheat noodles (soba) are also healthful and are available in Asian and health food stores.

Buckwheat Noodles

Serves: 6
Cooking time: 12 to 14 minutes
Preparation time: 10 minutes

- 7 ounces soba noodles (buckwheat, available in natural food stores)
- 2 bunches scallions
- 1 teaspoon sesame oil
- 2 tablespoons reduced-sodium soy sauce
- 2 tablespoons water
- Few dashes cayenne
- 1 teaspoon mustard
- 2 teaspoons toasted sesame seeds

Cook noodles according to package directions on conventional range top. When cooked to al dente, drain, turn into colander, and rinse quickly in cold water.

While noodles are cooking, trim roots and tops off scallions and slice lengthwise, then diagonally into 1-inch pieces. Place scallions in a 2-cup measure with sesame oil, and microwave on High for 1 minute. Add soy, water, cayenne, and mustard, and microwave on High another 1 minute. Turn noodles into a serving bowl, toss with sauce, and top with sesame seeds.

Per Serving: 0 Chol (mg); 23 Carbo (g); 3 Prot (g); 328 Na (mg)
Dietary Fiber: 4.6g **Fat (g):** 1; Sat .3; Poly .8; Mono .7 **Calories:** 143
Exchanges: 1½ starch/bread

Creamy Spinach Pasta

Serves: 4
Cooking time: 14 minutes
Preparation time: 5 minutes

  6 ounces spinach or whole wheat pasta
  2 tablespoons Parmesan or Romano cheese, grated
  ½ cup part-skim ricotta cheese
  ¼ cup non-fat plain yogurt
  1 tablespoon chives, chopped
  2 tablespoons walnuts, chopped

Cook pasta according to package directions on conventional range top to al dente. Drain and keep warm.

Meanwhile, place remaining ingredients, except walnuts, in a blender and process until creamy. Turn into a 2-cup measure and cover with paper towel. Microwave on High for 1 to 2 minutes, stirring, just until warm. Stir into pasta and top with walnuts.

Per Serving: 10 Chol (mg); 19 Carbo (g); 8 Prot (g); 102 Na (mg)
Dietary Fiber: 2.6g **Fat (g):** 4; Sat 1.9; Poly 1.0; Mono 1.1 **Calories:** 140
Exchanges: 1 starch/bread; 1 medium-fat meat

Green Noodles

Serves: 4
Cooking time: 15 to 17 minutes
Preparation time: 15 minutes

6 ounces spaghetti

1 teaspoon canola oil

4 cloves garlic, peeled and smashed

1 cup scallions, sliced, green tops included

¼ cup celery leaves, chopped

½ cup Chicken Broth (see index)

2 cups greens, shredded (chicory, romaine lettuce, spinach, escarole, or a combination)

1 tomato, sliced into thin wedges

1 tablespoon toasted pumpkin seeds

Cook noodles according to package directions on conventional range top. Drain when cooked.

Meanwhile, place oil, garlic, and scallions in a 2-quart measure, and microwave on High for 1 minute. Add celery leaves and chicken broth, and microwave on High another 2 minutes. Add shredded greens and stir to combine; microwave on High for another 1 minute.

Stir in cooked noodles, along with tomatoes, and microwave on High for 1 minute more until warmed through. Toss with pumpkin seeds.

Per Serving: 0 Chol (mg); 34 Carbo (g); 8 Prot (g); 115 Na (mg)
Dietary Fiber: 3.1g **Fat (g):** 3; Sat .4; Poly .8; Mono 1.2 **Calories:** 192
Exchanges: 2 starch/bread; 1 vegetable

Linguine with Clam Sauce

Serves: 6
Cooking time: 19 minutes
Preparation time: 20 minutes

8 ounces linguini

1 teaspoon olive oil

2 onions, finely chopped

3 cloves garlic, minced

¼ teaspoon dried oregano, crushed

¼ cup sliced water chestnuts, rinsed and drained

1 6½-ounce can whole baby clams, drained

½ cup fresh parsley, chopped

2 tablespoons white wine or vodka

Pepper to taste

Cook linguini according to package directions on conventional range top to al dente. Drain in colander.

While pasta is cooking, place oil, onions, and garlic in a 4-cup measure, and microwave on High for 3 to 4 minutes, stirring once. Add oregano and water chestnuts, and microwave on High 1 minute more.

Stir in clams, parsley, and wine or vodka, and microwave on High for 1 to 2 minutes, until warmed through. When pasta is cooked and drained, toss with sauce. Season with pepper to taste.

Per Serving: 21 Chol (mg); 34 Carbo (g); 13 Prot (g); 39 Na (mg)
Dietary Fiber: 2.6g **Fat (g):** 4; Sat .4; Poly .4; Mono 1.7 **Calories:** 228
Exchanges: 2 starch/bread; 1 lean meat

Pasta Pomadoro

Serves: 4
Cooking time: 12 minutes
Preparation time: 5 minutes

6 ounces spaghetti or ziti
6 ounces tomato sauce
¼ cup non-fat dry milk
2 scallions, chopped
¼ cup green peas
¼ teaspoon dried basil
   Pepper to taste

Cook pasta al dente according to package directions on conventional range top. In a bowl, mix together remaining ingredients. Cover with wax paper, and microwave on High for 2 to 3 minutes, until heated through. Stir to combine. Mix with spaghetti and serve.

Per Serving: 1 Chol (mg); 36 Carbo (g); 7 Prot (g); 305 Na (mg)
Dietary Fiber: 2.0g **Fat (g):** 1; Sat 0; Poly 0; Mono 0 **Calories:** 177
Exchanges: 2 starch/bread; 1 vegetable

Pignoli and Tomato Orzo

Serves: 4
Cooking time: 13 to 15 minutes
Preparation time: 10 minutes

> 1 teaspoon olive oil
> 1 tablespoon pine nuts (pignoli)
> ¼ cup sun-dried tomatoes
> Salt and pepper to taste
> 2 cups Chicken Broth (see index)
> 2 cups water
> ¾ cup orzo (small quill-shaped pasta)
> 1 tablespoon Romano or Parmesan cheese, grated

Soak dried tomatoes in boiling water until soft; drain and dice. Place pine nuts and tomatoes in a measuring cup with the oil. Microwave on High for 2 minutes, and season with salt and pepper. Let stand.

Bring the chicken broth and water to a boil by microwaving on High for about 5 minutes. Add orzo and microwave on High for 6 to 8 minutes, until tender. Drain and mix with pine nuts and tomatoes. Stir in grated cheese.

Per Serving: 2 Chol (mg); 20 Carbo (g); 7 Prot (g); 65 Na (mg)
Dietary Fiber: 1g **Fat (g):** 6; Sat 1.0; Poly 1.7; Mono 2.3 **Calories:** 151
Exchanges: 1 starch/bread; 1 fat

Red and Yellow Pepper Pasta

Serves: 4
Cooking time: 15 to 16 minutes
Preparation time: 10 minutes

6 ounces pasta (shells, rotelles, or angel hair)

1 pound red and yellow bell peppers, seeded and chopped (4 cups)

2 cloves garlic, minced

1 small red onion, quartered and sliced

1 teaspoon olive oil

2 tablespoons tomato paste diluted with ½ cup water

2 tablespoons chopped fresh basil or 1 teaspoon dried basil

2 tablespoons balsamic vinegar

Dash salt and pepper

Cook pasta according to package directions to al dente on conventional range top, drain, and keep warm.

Meanwhile, place peppers, garlic, onion, and olive oil in a 1-quart measure or casserole and microwave on High for 2 to 3 minutes, until tender. Stir.

Add tomato paste, basil, enough water to make a sauce, and vinegar. Microwave another 1 minute on High to warm. Combine with pasta and season with salt and pepper to taste.

Per Serving: 0 Chol (mg); 25 Carbo (g); 5 Prot (g); 105 Na (mg)
Dietary Fiber: 5.6g **Fat (g):** 2; Sat .3; Poly .5; Mono .8 **Calories:** 125
Exchanges: 1 starch/bread; 2 vegetables

Vegetable-Sauced Rotelles

Serves: 6
Cooking time: 16 minutes
Preparation time: 15 minutes

> 10 ounces dry rotelles (spirals), tomato and spinach flavored
> ½ red onion, chopped
> 1 medium green pepper, chopped
> 2 cloves garlic, minced
> 4 mushrooms, sliced
> 1 teaspoon olive oil
> ¼ teaspoon oregano
> ¼ to ½ teaspoon red pepper flakes
> 10 ounces tomato sauce
> 2 tablespoons part-skim mozzarella, shredded

Cook pasta at dente, according to package directions. Drain and set aside.

Mix next four ingredients with olive off in a 2-quart casserole, and microwave on High for 3 minutes. Add remaining ingredients, except cheese, cover with vented plastic wrap, and microwave on High for another 1 minute, until warm.

Mix in pasta and sprinkle with cheese. Microwave uncovered for about 40 seconds to 1 minute, until cheese is melted.

Per Serving: 3 Chol (mg); 42 Carbo (g); 10 Prot (g); 354 Na (mg)
Dietary Fiber: 7g **Fat (g):** 3; Sat .7; Poly .2; Mono .8 **Calories:** 226
Exchanges: 3 starch/bread; ½ fat

Vegetables

Mom was probably right to tell you to eat your spinach. She might well have just suggested the great span of fresh vegetables that are now available year round. Many of the recipes for leafy green vegetables—very high in calcium—can be interchanged: collards, mustard greens, kale, spinach, all may be prepared in similar ways. Carrots, fennel, beans, squash, cabbage, and turnips are all high in fiber and rich in nutrients. The addition to vegetable dishes of fresh herbs and spices as well as seeds and nuts provides more color, taste, and texture.

The microwave oven is a boon to vegetables; they are so quick to cook that none of the nutrients are lost, as in long cooking, and very little extra liquid is needed for their preparation. It is also a time-saver to cook the vegetables right in the very dishes you will use to serve them. No more pots to scrub!

When shopping for vegetables, select only brightly colored and unwilted greens and fresh, sturdy carrots, zucchini, peppers, fennel, and beans. Leafy green vegetables should be washed in tepid water to rid them of sand, then run under cold water. Any discolored leaves should be discarded.

While frozen vegetables are, in general, less desirable than fresh produce, some flash-frozen foods triumph, such as green peas and corn niblets. These need only be taken from the freezer and added to the recipe, as they will thaw in the cooking.

Acorn Squash

Serves: 4
Cooking time: 10 minutes
Preparation time: 5 minutes

> 2 acorn squash, about 1 ¼ pounds each (buttercup or butternut squash may also be used)
> 2 tablespoons non-fat plain yogurt
> Cinnamon
> Nutmeg
> Mace
> Black pepper
> 8 pecan halves, chopped

Pierce sides of each squash with fork. Wrap each in microwave-safe paper towel. Microwave on High for 5 minutes, turn, and microwave on High another 5 minutes. Remove paper, cut squash in half, and remove seeds and tough pulp. Place dollop of yogurt in each center, and sprinkle with a few dashes of the spices. Top with chopped pecans.

Per Serving: 0 Chol (mg); 16 Carbo (g); 2 Prot (g); 10 Na (mg)
Dietary Fiber: 5.2g **Fat (g):** 2; Sat .2; Poly .6; Mono 1.4 **Calories:** 84
Exchanges: 1 starch/bread

Bok Choy

Serves: 4
Cooking time: 3 to 4 minutes
Preparation time: 8 minutes

1 pound bok choy (Chinese celery), about 6 cups
1 teaspoon reduced-sodium soy sauce
1 clove garlic, minced
1 tablespoon frozen apple juice concentrate
 ½ teaspoon Sesame oil
 Dash ground ginger
1 tablespoon roasted pumpkin seeds

Chop bok choy into 1-inch slices and shred tops. Combine with remaining ingredients, except pumpkin seeds, and place in 2-quart glass measure or baking dish. Cover with vented plastic wrap, and microwave on High for 3 to 4 minutes, stirring once. Drain, toss with pumpkin seeds, and serve.

Per Serving: 0 Chol (mg); 6 Carbo (g); 5 Prot (g); 133 Na (mg)
Dietary Fiber: 7.3g **Fat (g):** 2; Sat .4; Poly 1.1; Mono .7 **Calories:** 58
Exchanges: 1 vegetable

Brussels Sprouts Almondine

Serves: 4
Cooking time: 7 to 9 minutes
Preparation time: 10 minutes

> 1 pound Brussels sprouts, cut in half
> ¼ cup Chicken Broth (see index)
> 1 clove garlic, minced
> 1 teaspoon whipped butter
> 1 teaspoon grainy Dijon mustard
> 1 tablespoon lemon juice
>   Dash pepper
> ¼ cup blanched almonds, slivered

Discard any discolored outer leaves, and rinse Brussels sprouts. Place in l-quart casserole or serving dish with chicken broth. Cover with wax paper and microwave on High for 3 to 4 minutes, stir, and microwave on High for another 3 to 4 minutes. Remove from oven and let rest a minute or two.

Meanwhile, combine remaining ingredients, and microwave on High for 40 seconds. Drain sprouts and toss with warmed sauce.

Per Serving: 0 Chol (mg); 9 Carbo (g); 3 Prot (g); 86 Na (mg)
Dietary Fiber: 4.3g **Fat (g):** 4; Sat .5; Poly 1.0; Mono 2.1 **Calories:** 68
Exchanges: 2 vegetable; 1 fat

Caraway Cabbage

Serves: 4
Cooking time: 10 to 12 minutes
Preparation time: 8 minutes

> 1 head green cabbage, about 1 to 1½ pounds
> 2 tablespoons frozen apple juice concentrate
> 2 tablespoons grainy Dijon mustard
> 4 drops sesame oil
> 1½ tablespoons caraway seeds

Trim stem off cabbage and cut into 8 wedges. Mix together remaining ingredients. Arrange cabbage wedges on their sides on a 12-inch glass baking dish, and coat with mustard mixture. Cover with vented plastic wrap, and microwave on High for 5 to 6 minutes. Rotate dish and microwave on High another 5 to 6 minutes, until crisp tender.

Per Serving: 0 Chol (mg); 7 Carbo (g); 1 Prot (g); 107 Na (mg)
Dietary Fiber: 1.6g **Fat (g):** .1; Sat 0; Poly 0; Mono 0 **Calories:** 34
Exchanges: 1 vegetable

Colorful Cauliflower

Serves: 4
Cooking time: 5 to 7 minutes
Preparation time: 10 minutes

   1 medium head cauliflower, about 1 pound, trimmed and cut into florets
1¼ cups green pepper, chopped
   1 medium carrot, finely diced
   1 teaspoon caraway seeds
  ¼ cup water
    Pepper

Place cauliflower in 1-quart casserole and sprinkle with green peppers, carrots, and caraway seeds. Add water, cover, and microwave on High for 5 to 7 minutes, stirring once. Dust with pepper to taste, and let stand 2 minutes before serving.

Per Serving: 0 Chol (mg); 7 Carbo (g); 2 Prot (g); 16 Na (mg)
Dietary Fiber: 3.5g **Fat (g):** 0; Sat 0; Poly 0; Mono 0 **Calories:** 32
Exchanges: 1 vegetable

Corn and Peppers

Serves: 4
Cooking time: 7 minutes
Preparation time: 10 minutes

½ cup green pepper, diced
½ cup red pepper, diced
1 teaspoon canola oil
2 cups corn niblets (canned or frozen and thawed)
¼ teaspoon ground cumin
¼ teaspoon chili powder
Dash powdered ginger
⅛ teaspoon pepper

Place green and red pepper in a 1-quart casserole with oil. Microwave on High for 3 minutes. Add remaining ingredients and cover with wax paper. Microwave on High for 4 minutes, stirring once mid-cycle.

Per Serving: 0 Chol (mg); 18 Carbo, (g); 3 Prot (g); 5 Na (mg)
Dietary Fiber: 3.9g **Fat (g):** 1; Sat .2; Poly .2; Mono .8 **Calories:** 82
Exchanges: 1 starch/bread

Green and Yellow Squash

Serves: 4
Cooking time: 4 to 6 minutes
Preparation time: 7 minutes

1 or 2 yellow squash, about ½ pound
1 or 2 zucchini, about ½ pound
2 ounces pimentos, drained and chopped
½ teaspoon dried oregano
1 bay leaf
2 cloves garlic, peeled and smashed
2 tablespoons lemon juice
1 teaspoon olive oil
1 tablespoon water
Pepper to taste
Chives, chopped

Rinse vegetables and trim. Cut squash and zucchini into thin slices. Combine all ingredients, except pepper and chives, in a 2-quart casserole. Stir to mix. Cover with vented plastic wrap and microwave on High for 2 to 3 minutes. Stir and microwave on High for another 2 to 3 minutes, until crisp-tender. Let stand covered for 2 minutes more. Remove bay leaf, sprinkle with pepper, and garnish with chopped chives.

Per Serving: 0 Chol (mg); 7 Carbo (g); 1 Prot (g); 4 Na (mg)
Dietary Fiber: 2.3g **Fat (g):** 1; Sat .2; Poly .2; Mono .8 **Calories:** 37
Exchanges: 1 vegetable

Hot Kale

Serves: 4
Cooking time: 9 to 12 minutes
Preparation time: 15 minutes

> 1 pound kale or turnip greens
> 1 cup Chicken Broth (see index)
> 1 cup water
> ½ teaspoon olive oil
> ¾ cup onion, chopped
> 3 cloves garlic, minced
> 1 tablespoon fresh ginger root, grated
> 3 to 4 leaves fresh basil (or ½ teaspoon dried)
> ½ teaspoon hot red pepper flakes
> 4 dashes sesame oil
> Juice of 1 lemon
> 1 teaspoon toasted pine nuts (pignoli)

Wash greens well in tepid water, and slice into thin strips. Place in 2-quart measure with broth, add water, cover with vented plastic wrap, and microwave on High 7 to 10 minutes, stirring once.

In a 2-cup measure, place the oil, onion, garlic, ginger, basil, and pepper flakes, and microwave on High for 2 minutes. Drain greens, stir in onion mixture, and complete seasoning with sesame oil and lemon juice. Garnish with pine nuts.

Per Serving: 0 Chol (mg); 7 Carbo (g); 4 Prot (g); 204 Na (mg)
Dietary Fiber: 3.7g **Fat (g):** 2; Sat .2; Poly .4; Mono .8 **Calories:** 48
Exchanges: 1 vegetable

Hot Peppered Greens

Serves: 4
Cooking time: 3 to 5 minutes
Preparation time: 10 minutes

- 1 pound fresh kale, collard greens, beet tops, or mustard greens
- 1 tablespoon red pepper flakes
- 3 cloves garlic, peeled and mashed
- 1 cup water
- Juice of 1 lemon
- Pinch salt
- 1 tablespoon sunflower seeds

Chop greens and mix all ingredients together, except sunflower seeds, in a 2-quart measure. Cover with wax paper. Microwave on High for 3 to 5 minutes, stirring once during cycle. Serve with sprinkling of sunflower seeds.

Per Serving: 0 Chol (mg); 6 Carbo (g); 2 Prot (g); 85 Na (mg)
Dietary Fiber: 3.3g **Fat (g):** 1; Sat. 1; Poly .7; Mono .2 **Calories:** 38
Exchanges: 1 vegetable

Okra Provençal

Serves: 6
Cooking time: 8 to 10 minutes
Preparation time: 15 minutes

    1 pound small fresh okra pods, trimmed
    1 12-ounce can stewed tomatoes, drained and crushed
    4 scallions, chopped
    2 cloves garlic, minced
    ½ cup green pepper, chopped
    8 small pimento-stuffed olives
    ¼ cup parsley, chopped
      Pinch each of dried thyme and marjoram
    2 teaspoons dried basil
      Salt and pepper to taste

Place okra pods on paper towels in an 8 x 12-inch baking dish. Microwave on High for 2 to 3 minutes, until tender, turning once.

Place remaining ingredients in a 1-quart measure and cover with wax paper. Microwave on High for 5 to 6 minutes. Stir, and add okra pods. Microwave together for 1 minute on High to heat through. Stir and serve.

Per Serving: 0 Chol (mg); 13 Carbo (g); 3 Prot (g); 181 Na (mg)
Dietary Fiber: 4.1g **Fat (g):** 2; Sat .2; Poly .6; Mono .3 **Calories:** 60
Exchanges: 2 vegetable

Pimento Asparagus

Serves: 4
Cooking time: 6 to 7 minutes
Preparation time: 5 minutes

> 1¼ pounds fresh asparagus
> 2 tablespoons fresh lemon juice
> 2 tablespoons pimentos, chopped
> 1 tablespoon toasted pine nuts (pignoli)

Snap ends off asparagus and rime. Arrange on platter in single layer. Drizzle on lemon juice, and sprinkle pimento pieces on top. Cover with wax paper.

Microwave on High for 5 to 6 minutes, turning dish once during cycle. Cook another minute or so if softer spears are desired. Toss pine nuts over asparagus and serve.

Per Serving: 0 Chol (mg); 7 Carbo (g); 3 Prot (g); 6 Na (mg)
Dietary Fiber: 3.5g **Fat (g):** 2; Sat .3; Poly .7; Mono .5 **Calories:** 37
Exchanges: 1 vegetable

Pine Nut Green Beans

Serves: 4
Cooking time: 7 to 9 minutes
Preparation time: 10 minutes

> 1 pound fresh green beans, trimmed and washed
> ½ cup Italian plum tomatoes, drained and crushed
> 2 tablespoons toasted pine nuts (pignoli)
>   Dash pepper

Place green beans and tomatoes in an 8-inch baking dish or casserole and stir to mix. Cover with lid or wax paper. Microwave on High for 7 to 9 minutes or until tender, stirring twice. Drain off any excess liquid, toss with pine nuts, and season with pepper.

Per Serving: 0 Chol (mg); 7 Carbo (g); 3 Prot (g); 51 Na (mg)
Dietary Fiber: 2.3g **Fat (g):** 3; Sat .4; Poly 1.2; Mono 1.0 **Calories:** 53
Exchanges: 1 vegetable; ½ fat

Ratatouille

Serves: 8
Cooking time: 25 minutes
Preparation time: 15 to 20 minutes

1 small eggplant, cubed

1 onion, chopped

6 cloves garlic, peeled and smashed

1 tablespoon olive oil

2 cups tomatoes, cubed (cherry tomatoes, halved, are fine)

1 medium zucchini or yellow squash, sliced

2 tablespoons chopped fresh basil or ½ teaspoon dried basil

1 teaspoon dried thyme

1 teaspoon dried oregano

Salt and pepper to taste

1 medium red bell pepper, cut into 1-inch squares

1 medium green or yellow bell pepper, cut into 1-inch squares

1 teaspoon hot red pepper flakes

In a 2-quart measure or casserole, place eggplant, onion, garlic, and oil. Microwave on High for 10 minutes, stirring once or twice. Add tomatoes, zucchini, and spices and microwave on High 10 minutes, stirring once. Add peppers and hot pepper flakes and microwave another 5 minutes on High. Stir to blend. Let rest before serving warm or chilled.

Per Serving: 0 Chol (mg); 8 Carbo (g); 1 Prot (g); 21 Na (mg)
Dietary Fiber: 2.5g **Fat (g):** 2; Sat .3; Poly .3; Mono 1.3 **Calories:** 48
Exchanges: 1 vegetable

Ruby Red Cabbage

Serves: 6
Cooking time: 11 minutes
Preparation time: 15 minutes

1 medium onion
4 cloves garlic, peeled and minced
2 teaspoons canola oil
½ pound red cabbage, shredded (about 4 cups)
¼ cup balsamic vinegar
2 tablespoons frozen orange juice concentrate
1 cup Chicken Broth (see index)
3 tablespoons raisins
1 tablespoon ginger root, finely chopped
½ teaspoon cloves, powdered
1 bay leaf
Juice of 1 lemon

Place onion, garlic, and oil in 2-quart casserole or measuring cup, and microwave on High for 3 minutes. Mix with shredded cabbage and remaining ingredients, cover with wax paper, and microwave on High for 4 minutes. Stir, and microwave on High for another 4 minutes. When cabbage is tender, discard bay leaf.

Per Serving: 1 Chol (mg); 9 Carbo (g); 2 Prot (g); 193 Na (mg)
Dietary Fiber: 3.8g **Fat (g):** 3; Sat .6; Poly 1.8; Mono .9 **Calories:** 99
Exchanges: 2 vegetable

Rutabaga Mousse

Serves: 6
Cooking time: 21 minutes
Preparation time: 10 minutes

> 1 rutabaga, about 1 ½ pounds
> ½ cup water
> ⅛ teaspoon nutmeg, grated
> ¼ teaspoon cinnamon, ground
> ½ teaspoon celery seed
> 4 tablespoons non-fat dry milk
> 1 tablespoon part-skim ricotta cheese
> ¼ cup frozen apple juice concentrate
> 2 tablespoons parsley, chopped, for garnish

Peel and dice rutabaga and place in 2-quart measure with water. Cover with vented plastic wrap, and microwave on High for 20 minutes, until tender. Turn into food processor, reserving some cooking liquid if needed later to thin.

Add all remaining ingredients, except parsley, and process to blend. Microwave on High for 30 to 40 seconds until warm. Garnish with parsley.

Per Serving: 2 Chol (mg); 9 Carbo (g); 3 Prot (g); 49 Na (mg)
Dietary Fiber: 1.7g **Fat (g):** 1; Sat .2; Poly .1; Mono .1 **Calories:** 69
Exchanges: 2 vegetable

Sesame Spinach

Serves: 4
Cooking time: 6 to 8 minutes
Preparation time: 10 minutes

- 1 teaspoon sesame oil
- 2 cloves garlic, minced
- ½ onion, chopped
- 1½ pounds fresh spinach
- 1 teaspoon reduced-sodium soy sauce
- ⅛ teaspoon fresh ginger root, minced
- 2 tablespoons sliced water chestnuts, rinsed and drained
- 2 teaspoons toasted sesame seeds

Place oil in measuring cup with garlic and onion, and microwave on High for 1 minute, until tender. Wash spinach well and cut off tough stems; place it in 4-quart casserole with just the water left on the leaves. Cover with vented plastic wrap, and microwave on High for 4 to 6 minutes, stirring once, until wilted.

Drain spinach, mix with onion and garlic mixture, add soy, ginger root, and water chestnuts, and microwave on High 1 more minute. Toss with sesame seeds and serve. This is also nice as a salad if served chilled.

Per Serving: 0 Chol (mg); 9 Carbo (g); 6 Prot (g); 189 Na (mg)
Dietary Fiber: 1.4g **Fat (g):** 3; Sat .4; Poly 1.0; Mono .8 **Calories:** 65
Exchanges: 2 vegetable; ½ fat

Sesame Eggplant

Serves: 4
Cooking time: 4 to 6 minutes
Preparation time: 20 minutes

1 medium eggplant, about 1½ pounds
2 stalks fresh asparagus (or 1 cup broccoli)
3 tablespoons carrot, chopped
½ teaspoon dried basil
2 cloves garlic, peeled
1 tablespoon olive oil
½ teaspoon sesame oil
1 tablespoon toasted sesame seeds
Salt and pepper to taste

Peel eggplant and chop into 1-inch pieces. Cut asparagus or broccoli into small pieces. Combine all ingredients, except sesame seeds and salt and pepper. Place in large bowl and cover with wax paper.

Microwave on High for 2 to 3 minutes. Turn bowl and stir. Microwave on High another 2 to 3 minutes. Stir, adding sesame seeds and seasoning.

Per Serving: 0 Chol (mg); 11 Carbo (g); 4 Prot (g); 15 Na (mg)
Dietary Fiber: 3.9g **Fat (g):** 5; Sat .8; Poly 1.2; Mono 3.2 **Calories:** 95
Exchanges: 2 vegetable; 1 fat

Spaghetti Squash

Serves: 4
Cooking time: 25 to 26 minutes
Preparation time: 9 minutes

> 1 spaghetti squash, about 2 pounds
> 1 tablespoon olive oil
> 1 cup mushrooms, sliced
> 2 tablespoons scallions, chopped
> Pepper

Pierce squash on sides with fork. Place in microwave on double layer of microwave-safe paper towels. Microwave on High for 5 minutes. Turn and microwave on High another 5 minutes. Cut squash in half and discard seeds. Cover each half with wax paper, and microwave an additional 12 to 13 minutes on High, until tender, rotating twice. Let stand 3 minutes.

Meanwhile, place olive oil, sliced mushrooms, and scallions in 4-cup measure, and microwave on High, uncovered, for 3 minutes. Stir.

Uncover squash and, with fork, scrape spaghetti strands into a bowl. Top with mushrooms and scallions, season with pepper, and serve. Squash may also be served chilled. (Spaghetti squash is also nice served with tomato sauce or salsa topping.)

Per Serving: 0 Chol (mg); 9 Carbo (g); 1 Prot (g); 22 Na (mg)
Dietary Fiber: 2.5g **Fat (g):** 4; Sat .5; Poly .5; Mono 2.5 **Calories:** 70
Exchanges: 2 vegetable; 1 fat

Vegetable Mélange

Serves: 4
Cooking time: 3 to 5 minutes
Preparation time: 15 minutes

> 1 cup broccoli florets
> 1 cup cauliflower florets
> ½ cup carrots, sliced into thin rounds
> ½ cup red bell pepper, sliced
> 1 cup snow peas, trimmed
> ½ cup fresh bean sprouts
> 2 tablespoons lemon juice
> 1 tablespoon chives, chopped
>   Pepper

Arrange vegetables in 10-inch baking dish or serving platter. Place broccoli and cauliflower in a circle on outside, with a ring of carrots and red peppers inside of circle. Mound bean sprouts in center and surround with snow peas.

Sprinkle vegetables with lemon juice and cover with wax paper. Microwave on High for 3 to 5 minutes, until vegetables are crisp-tender. Let stand covered for 3 minutes; then remove paper. Sprinkle with chives and dash of pepper.

Any combination of vegetables may be substituted, according to availability or choice. Use zucchini or summer squash slices, asparagus, turnips, wax or green beans. Always place softer vegetables in center of arrangement.

Per Serving: 0 Chol (mg); 11 Carbo (g); 5 Prot (g); 20 Na (mg)
Dietary Fiber: 4.9g **Fat (g):** 0; Sat 0; Poly 0; Mono 0 **Calories:** 57
Exchanges: 2 vegetable

Sauces

Sauces add a little something extra to nearly everything. Depending upon your tastes, they may be used to top grains or pasta, potatoes, vegetables, poultry, fish, or even desserts. Some sauces may also be used as dips for pre-meal teasers. Inventive cooks can combine whatever they like, using non-fat milk or yogurt or low-fat cottage cheese, tomato and vegetable combinations pureed, and even peanut butter or nuts. Experimenting and experiencing taste treats is fun.

Caper Sauce

Serves: 4 (2-tablespoon servings)
Cooking time: 1 minute
Preparation time: 2 minutes

¼ cup non-fat plain yogurt
1 tablespoon capers, rinsed and drained
1 teaspoon Dijon mustard
2 teaspoons parsley, chopped
⅛ teaspoon paprika
⅛ teaspoon pepper

Combine all ingredients in 1-cup measure, and microwave on High for 30 seconds to 1 minute, just until warm. Spoon over poached fish, such as salmon, or poultry.

Per Serving: 0 Chol (mg); 1 Carbo (g); 1 Prot (g); 27 Na (mg)
Dietary Fiber: 0g **Fat (g):** 0; Sat 0; Poly 0; Mono 0 **Calories:** 7
Exchanges: free

Cranberry and Orange Sauce

Serves: 16 (2-tablespoon servings)
Cooking time: 5 minutes
Preparation time: 7 minutes

- 1 12-ounce package fresh cranberries
- ¼ cup frozen orange juice concentrate
- 1 orange
- 2 tablespoons walnuts, chopped

Wash cranberries and discard any debris. Combine in a 1-quart casserole or measure with orange juice. Cover with vented plastic wrap, and microwave on High 5 minutes, until soft. Cut the orange into quarters, then eighths.

Let cranberries cool a bit before turning half of them into a food processor with half of the orange sections. Puree and pour into serving bowl. Process remaining cranberries and oranges and add to serving bowl. Chill before serving, and garnish with chopped walnuts. Makes 2 cups.

Per Serving: 0 Chol (mg); 5 Carbo (g); 0 Prot (g); 0 Na (mg)
Dietary Fiber: 1.0g **Fat (g):** 0; Sat 0; Poly 0; Mono 0 **Calories:** 21
Exchanges: free

Lemon Sauce

Serves: 16 (2-tablespoon servings)
Cooking time: 2 minutes
Preparation time: 5 minutes

> 1 lemon, washed, trimmed, and cut into pieces
> 1 cup soft tofu (bean curd)
> Few dashes sesame oil
> ¼ cup non-fat plain yogurt
> 1 teaspoon horseradish
> 1 teaspoon Dijon mustard
> ¼ teaspoon salt
> Fresh pepper to taste
> 1 teaspoon black olives, chopped (optional)

Blend all ingredients, except olives, in a food processor and turn into a 4-cup measure. Microwave on High for 2 minutes, stirring once. Top with chopped olives if desired. Serve over pasta, grains, or fish or use as an appetizer dip with crudites. It's even good served on a dessert! Makes 2 cups.

Per Serving: 0 Chol (mg); 0 Carbo (g); 1 Prot (g); 20 Na (mg)
Dietary Fiber: 0g **Fat (g):** 0; Sat. 1; Poly .2; Mono. 1 **Calories:** 6
Exchanges: free

Saucy Salsa

Serves: 4 (as sauce)
Cooking time: 3½ to 5 minutes
Preparation time: 10 minutes

> 3 cloves garlic, minced
> ½ cup onion, chopped
> 4 ounces tomato puree
> 4 ounces fresh ripe tomatoes, chopped, or canned Italian plum tomatoes, drained and crushed
> 1 fresh green chili, chopped
> ½ teaspoon ground cumin
> ½ teaspoon dried oregano

Place garlic and onion in l-quart glass measure, and microwave on High for 1 ½ to 2 minutes. Add remaining ingredients and cover with plastic wrap. Microwave on High for 2 to 3 minutes and stir to blend.

Per Serving: 0 Chol (mg); 6 Carbo (g); 1 Prot (g); 128 Na (mg)
Dietary Fiber: .8g **Fat (g):** 0; Sat 0; Poly 0; Mono 0 **Calories:** 27
Exchanges: 1 vegetable

Spinach Sauce

Serves: 12 (2-tablespoon servings)
Cooking time: 2 to 3 minutes
Preparation time: 10 minutes

- ½ pound fresh spinach, trimmed of tough stems, well washed
- ½ tablespoon olive oil
- 1 tablespoon oat bran
- Pepper to taste
- ⅛ teaspoon ground nutmeg
- ¼ teaspoon ground cardamom
- 1 tablespoon lemon juice
- ½ cup non-fat plain yogurt at room temperature

Place wet spinach in a 2-quart casserole or measure, and microwave on High for 1 to 2 minutes, until wilted. Puree in food processor or blender with all remaining ingredients except yogurt.

Return to casserole and microwave on High for another 1 minute, stirring. Blend in yogurt and adjust seasoning. Serve over fish, poultry, pasta, or rice or use as an appetizer dip.

Per Serving: 1 Chol (mg); 4 Carbo (g); 3 Prot (g); 70 Na (mg)
Dietary Fiber: 1.7g **Fat (g):** 2; Sat .3; Poly .2; Mono 1.3 **Calories:** 40
Exchanges: 1 vegetable

Walnut Sauce

Serves: 5 (2-tablespoon servings)
Cooking time: 1 to 2 minutes
Preparation time: 5 minutes

½ cup walnuts or pecans, shelled
1 teaspoon Dijon mustard
1 teaspoon olive oil
2 to 3 tablespoons fresh lemon juice
1 teaspoon whole wheat bread crumbs
1 tablespoon frozen apple juice concentrate

Chop nuts in food processor, then add remaining ingredients and puree. Place in 2-cup measure, and microwave on High for 1 to 2 minutes to warm through. Serve over fish or poultry or even pasta or potatoes. This sauce is also tasty enough to be used as an appetizer, spreading a little on an endive leaf or cracker.

Per Serving: 0 Chol (mg); 4 Carbo (g); 1 Prot (g); 17 Na (mg)
Dietary Fiber: .9g **Fat (g):** 8; Sat .7; Poly 1.8; Mono 5 **Calories:** 99
Exchanges: 2 fat

Yogurt Sour Cream

Serves: 16 (1-tablespoon servings)
Cooking time: 0
Preparation time: 2 minutes plus refrigerating time

2 cups non-fat plain yogurt
Flavors as desired (see below)

Place yogurt in a cheesecloth or coffee-filter-lined sieve, and let drip over a bowl in the refrigerator for 4 to 6 hours or overnight, until the yogurt has the consistency of thick sour cream. Makes 1 cup.

Flavored Yogurt Sour Cream

For a sweet flavor, add cinnamon, vanilla extract, or frozen orange juice concentrate. For savory tastes, add herbs such as dill, tarragon, parsley, oregano, or caraway before placing yogurt in sieve.

Per Serving: 1 Chol (mg); 3 Carbo (g); 2 Prot (g); 0 Na (mg)
Dietary Fiber: 0g **Fat (g):** 0; Sat 0; Poly 0; Mono 0 **Calories:** 22
Exchanges: free

Baked Goods

Everything I had read told me that you just can't bake in a microwave oven. Wrong! Much to my delight, I discovered that you can bake quickly and efficiently in a microwave. I tried some of my favorite breads and muffins and found that they came out just as tasteful and in less time than when using a conventional oven. The baked goods do not have a browned top, but that is readily overcome by dusting the top with poppy or caraway seeds or paprika and running them under the conventional broiler for a few seconds. The results are well worth the paler look.

Banana Bread

Serves: 12 (1 slice each)
Cooking time: 12–15 minutes
Preparation time: 30 minutes plus cooling time

Non-stick vegetable spray
1½ cups all-purpose unbleached flour
¼ cup rye flour
1½ teaspoons baking powder
½ teaspoon baking soda
¼ teaspoon salt
½ teaspoon powdered ginger
1 cup ripe banana, mashed (about 2 medium bananas)
1 tablespoon lemon juice
3 tablespoons frozen orange juice concentrate
⅓ cup I Can't Believe It's Not Butter
2 eggs (1 yolk only)
⅓ cup evaporated skim milk
½ cup pecans or walnuts, chopped
2 tablespoons plus 1 teaspoon currants
Few dashes cinnamon

Coat the bottom of a 9 x 5-inch glass loaf pan with non-stick vegetable spray. In a bowl, mix together the flours, baking powder, baking soda, salt, and ginger. In another small bowl, mash bananas, mix with lemon juice, and set aside.

In a large bowl, combine the orange juice, I Can't Believe It's Not Butter, eggs, and milk. Stir in chopped nuts and 2 tablespoons currants. Fold in mashed bananas and add dry ingredients, mixing well. Turn into baking dish and top with 1 teaspoon currants and a few dashes of cinnamon.

Place in microwave oven on inverted saucer. Microwave on Medium High (70%) for 3 ½ to 4 minutes. Turn pan and continue microwaving at 70% for another 3 ½ to 4 minutes. Microwave on High for 4 to 5 minutes, until a knife inserted into the center of the bread comes out clean.

If a browned top is desired, place under conventional oven broiler for 30 seconds. Let cool 10 minutes. Remove from pan. If bottom is still damp, return to microwave, bottom up, and microwave on High for 1 to 2 minutes, until no longer wet.

This bread gets better after refrigeration for a day (if it's not all eaten!).

Per Serving: 23 Chol (mg); 23 Carbo (g); 4 Prot (g); 169 Na (mg)
Dietary Fiber: 1.8g **Fat (g):** 6; Sat 1; Poly 1.7; Mono 3.3 **Calories:** 161
Exchanges: 1 ½ starch/bread; 1 fat

Blueberry Cobbler

∙∙∙

Serves: 8
Cooking time: 8 to 10 minutes
Preparation time: 15 minutes

2 cups fresh blueberries
⅓ cup whole wheat flour
⅓ cup unbleached all-purpose flour
1 teaspoon baking soda
3 tablespoons frozen orange juice concentrate
1 cup non-fat plain yogurt
1 teaspoon poppy seeds

Wash blueberries and pick over, discarding any debris. Turn into an 8-inch-square baking dish.

Mix together the flours and baking soda. Stir in orange juice and yogurt and when blended, pour over berries. Sprinkle poppy seeds over dough and place in oven on an inverted saucer.

Microwave on High for 4 to 5 minutes. Rotate dish and microwave on High another 4 to 5 minutes. Cobbler is done when it springs back when touched lightly. Top with blend of cottage cheese and part-skim ricotta if desired.

∙∙∙

Per Serving: 1 Chol (mg); 15 Carbo (g); 3 Prot (g); 127 Na (mg)
Dietary Fiber: 1.8g **Fat (g):** 0; Sat 0; Poly 0; Mono 0 **Calories:** 72
Exchanges: 1 starch/bread

Buttermilk Soda Bread

Serves: 16 (1 slice each)
Cooking time: 12 to 13 minutes
Preparation time: 15 minutes plus cooling time

> 1 cup rye flour
> 1 cup unbleached all-purpose flour
> ¼ cup wheat germ
> 1 teaspoon baking soda
> 2 teaspoons double-acting baking powder
> ½ teaspoon salt
> 2 cups buttermilk
> 2 tablespoons canola oil
> 2 tablespoons sunflower seeds
> 2 tablespoons currants
> Non-stick vegetable spray
> Poppy seeds

In a large bowl, mix together the first six ingredients. In another bowl, combine buttermilk and canola oil, and then stir into flour mixture and blend. Add sunflower seeds and currants, and turn into an 8 x 10-inch baking dish coated with non-stick spray. Top with a few dashes of poppy seeds, and place dish on inverted saucer in oven.

Microwave on High for 5 minutes. Rotate dish and microwave on High another 7 to 8 minutes. Bread is done when toothpick inserted comes out clean or top springs back when touched. Remove and let cool.

Per Serving: 1 Chol (mg); 14 Carbo (g); 4 Prot (g); 123 Na (mg)
Dietary Fiber: 1.4g **Fat (g):** 3; Sat .5; Poly 5; Mono 1.4 **Calories:** 92
Exchanges: 1 starch/bread; ½ fat

Confetti Corn Muffins

Serves: 12 (1 muffin each)
Cooking time: 4 to 5½ minutes
Preparation time: 15 minutes

½ cup all-purpose unbleached flour

½ cup rye flour

½ cup yellow cornmeal

1 tablespoon baking soda

¼ teaspoon salt

1 teaspoon dried oregano

1 teaspoon chili powder

1 tablespoon frozen orange juice concentrate

2 eggs (1 yolk only), beaten

1 tablespoon vegetable oil

¾ cup canned corn niblets, drained (if frozen, thawed)

⅔ cup skim milk

⅓ cup green pepper, diced

⅓ cup red onion, chopped

Mix all ingredients together and spoon into 12 muffin cups, using paper liners. Fill each cup half full. Microwave on High for 4 to 5½ minutes, rotating and rearranging mid-cycle. If making 6 muffins at a time, cook 3 to 4½ minutes. Muffins are baked when they spring back if poked gently. Makes 12 muffins.

Timing

2 muffins = ½ to 2 minutes

4 muffins = 1 to 2½ minutes

6 muffins = 3 to 4½ minutes

12 muffins = 4 to 5½ minutes

Note: If you do not have a microwave-safe muffin tin, try using paper hot cups cut off half-way.

Per Serving: 23 Chol (mg); 17 Carbo (g); 4 Prot (g); 295 Na (mg)
Dietary Fiber: 2.3g **Fat (g):** 2; Sat .4; Poly .9; Mono .5 **Calories:** 97
Exchanges: 1 starch/bread

Currant Scones

Serves: 8 (1 scone each)
Cooking time: 7 minutes
Preparation time: 20 minutes plus cooling time

- ½ cup all-purpose unbleached flour
- ¼ cup whole wheat flour
- ¼ cup yellow cornmeal
- 1½ teaspoons baking powder
- ¼ teaspoon salt
- 1 tablespoon whipped butter
- 1 tablespoon canola oil
- ¼ cup part-skim mozzarella, shredded, or other low-fat cheese
- ½ teaspoon maple extract
- 2 egg whites
- ⅓ cup skim milk
- 2 teaspoons caraway seeds
- 2 tablespoons currants
- Paprika
- Non-stick spray

In a large bowl, combine flours, cornmeal, baking powder, and salt. Stir in butter, oil, and cheese, until mixture is crumbly. Beat the egg whites and milk with maple extract and stir into flour mixture. Add caraway seeds and currants and blend.

Dust a board with flour and knead the dough into a ball. Roll into a 7-inch circle and cut into 8 even wedges. Dust tops of each wedge with a little paprika.

Coat a 9-inch pie plate with non-stick spray and arrange wedges on plate. Place pie plate on inverted saucer in the oven, and microwave on Medium (50%) for 6 minutes, until puffy, rotating pie plate every 2 minutes. Turn scones over and microwave on bottom side for 1 minute more at 50% power.

Let cool. Serve with a dollop of part-skim ricotta or a little sugar-free fruit preserve if desired. Makes 8 scones.

Per Serving: 7 Chol (mg); 14 Carbo (g); 5 Prot (g); 181 Na (mg)
Dietary Fiber: 1.2g **Fat (g):** 4; Sat 1.6; Poly .3; Mono 1.9 **Calories:** 113
Exchanges: 1 starch/bread; 1 fat

Golden Carrot Muffins

Serves: 12 (1 muffin each)
Cooking time: 10 to 11 minutes (2 batches)
Preparation time: 15 minutes

 1 cup all bran (sugar free)
 ¾ cup skim milk
 4 carrots, shredded (about 2 cups)
1 to 1½ cups whole wheat flour
 2 tablespoons frozen orange juice concentrate
 2 tablespoons canola oil
 1 tablespoon fresh lemon juice
 1 tablespoon sunflower seeds
 1 teaspoon baking powder
 1 teaspoon baking soda
 1 teaspoon ground cinnamon
 ½ teaspoon ground ginger
 ⅛ teaspoon salt
 1 egg, beaten
 1 tablespoon unsweetened coconut, shredded

In a 2-quart bowl, combine bran with milk and shredded carrots (shred the carrots in a food processor to save time). Let stand for 5 minutes while mixing all remaining ingredients, except coconut.

Line a microwave-safe muffin tin with 2 paper liners (or use cut-off paper hot cups instead), and fill each cup half-way. Top each muffin with a sprinkle of coconut.

Microwave on High for 5 to 5½ minutes, until muffins are springy when touched. Makes 12 muffins. It is best to microwave 6 muffins at a time.

Per Serving: 23 Chol (mg); 19 Carbo (g); 4 Prot (g); 181 Na (mg)
Dietary Fiber: 4.4g **Fat (g):** 4; Sat .7; Poly .6; Mono 1.9 **Calories:** 112
Exchanges: 1 starch/bread; 1 fat

Gourmet Cheese Muffins

Serves: 12 (1 muffin each)
Cooking time: 8 to 10 minutes (2 batches)
Preparation time: 15 minutes

    1 cup buttermilk
    1 egg
1½ tablespoons canola oil
    1 cup all-purpose unbleached flour
    ¼ cup whole wheat flour
    1 teaspoon baking powder
    ½ teaspoon baking soda
    ¼ teaspoon salt
    6 tablespoons Parmesan cheese, grated
    ½ teaspoon dried rosemary, crushed
       Non-stick vegetable spray

Beat together the buttermilk, egg, and oil. In another large bowl, sift together the flours, baking powder, soda, and salt.

Combine grated cheese and rosemary in a separate dish and mix. Add 5 tablespoons of it to flour mixture and blend. Pour buttermilk mixture into flour and combine.

Coat a microwave-safe muffin dish with vegetable spray. Turn batter into cups (filling each about ⅔ full), and top each one with some of the Parmesan-rosemary blend. Place in oven on an inverted saucer and microwave on High for 4 to 5 minutes (rotating once), until either a toothpick inserted in the center comes out clean or muffins spring back when touched.

Muffin tin probably has room for only 6 muffins, so repeat when first batch is finished. If a microwave-safe muffin pan is hard to find, use cut-off paper hot cups instead. Makes 12 muffins.

Per Serving: 26 Chol (mg); 12 Carbo (g); 4 Prot (g); 171 Na (mg)
Dietary Fiber: .6g **Fat (g):** 3; Sat 1.0; Poly .3; Mono 1.7 **Calories:** 92
Exchanges: 1 starch/bread; ½ fat

Oat Bran Muffins

Serves: 12 (1 muffin each)
Cooking time: 10 to 12 minutes (2 batches)
Preparation time: 10 minutes

2½ cups oat bran
2 tablespoons raisins
1 teaspoon baking powder
½ teaspoon orange peel, grated
Few dashes ground ginger
¼ teaspoon cinnamon
⅛ teaspoon salt
¼ cup almonds (or walnuts), halved
¾ cup buttermilk
¼ cup plus 2 tablespoons frozen orange juice concentrate
2 eggs (1 yolk only)
2 tablespoons canola oil

Mix dry ingredients, except almonds or walnuts, together in a large bowl, and mix the remaining ingredients in another. Combine both mixtures well and turn into microwave-safe muffin tin lined with double paper liners (or use paper hot cups cut off to about 1½ inches). Top each with a nut, and microwave 6 muffins at a time on High for 5 to 6 minutes, rotating once. Muffins are done when springy to the touch or an inserted toothpick comes out clean. Makes 12 muffins.

Per Serving: 23 Chol (mg); 16 Carbo (g); 6 Prot (g); 74 Na (mg)
Dietary Fiber: 4.4g **Fat (g):** 6; Sat 1.5; Poly 1.4; Mono 3.1 **Calories:** 126
Exchanges: 1 starch/bread; 1 fat

Desserts

I have always had a preference for a simple piece of fruit to finish off a good meal. But many people crave something more elaborate as a dessert, particularly when other people without diabetes share a meal. The microwave does a good job of whipping up delectable desserts in short order. Many of these recipes are fruit-based, and many use low-fat milk or yogurt and even grains and potatoes.

Fruit is the natural sweetener in all the recipes, so fear of too much sugar is never an issue.

To have berries or melon on hand when they are not in season, try freezing them on a cookie sheet and then storing them in small quantities in plastic freezer bags. Blackberries, strawberries, raspberries, and blueberries may all be kept frozen and used to make dessert dressings or toppings throughout the year. Melon may be scooped into small rounds or cut into chunks and frozen in the same way.

Apricot Prune Whip

Serves; 4
Cooking time: 2 to 3 minutes
Preparation time: 6 minutes

  ½ cup water
  ½ cup dried apricots
  ½ cup prunes, pitted
  1 cup soft tofu (bean curd)
  2 teaspoons pure vanilla extract
  2 tablespoons non-fat dry milk
  4 medium strawberries (or raspberries)

Place water, apricots, and prunes in 2-cup glass measure, and microwave on High for 2 to 3 minutes, until soft. Let cool. Place fruit in food processor with remaining ingredients, except berries, and whip until smooth. Serve warm or chilled, topped with strawberries for garnish.

Per Serving: 0 Chol (mg); 17 Carbo (g); 6 Prot (g); 18 Na (mg)
Dietary Fiber: 4.7g **Fat (g):** 3; Sat .5; Poly 1.6; Mono .7 **Calories:** 110
Exchanges: 1 fruit; 1 lean meat

Betty's Baked Apples

Serves: 4
Cooking time: 5 to 6 minutes
Preparation time: 10 minutes

> 4 McIntosh apples, cored
> 2 tablespoons raisins
> 2 tablespoons sunflower seeds
> 2 teaspoons powdered cinnamon
> 2 tablespoons frozen apple juice concentrate
> 1 tablespoon water

Peel away about ½ inch of skin from top of apples and pierce with a fork in several places. Fill cores with raisins, sunflower seeds, a few dashes of cinnamon, and a dab of apple juice. Place in deep baking dish, add water, and cover with vented plastic wrap. Microwave on High for 5 to 6 minutes, turning dish once. Spoon sauce over apples and serve warm or chilled.

Per Serving: 0 Chol (mg); 23 Carbo (g); 1 Prot (g); 2 Na (mg)
Dietary Fiber: 2.5g **Fat (g):** 2; Sat .3; Poly 1.4; Mono .4 **Calories:** 109
Exchanges: 1½ fruit

Buttercup Cream

Serves: 4
Cooking time: 4 to 5 minutes
Preparation time: 10 minutes plus cooling time

> 1 buttercup or butternut squash, about 1 ¼ pounds
> 2 tablespoons part-skim ricotta cheese
> 2 tablespoons non-fat dry milk
> 1 tablespoon frozen orange juice concentrate
> Dash cinnamon
> Dash nutmeg
> 1 tablespoon almonds, slivered

Pierce squash with a fork in several places. Arrange over two layers of microwave-safe paper towels, and microwave on High for 4 to 5 minutes, turning once. When soft, cut in half, discard seeds, and scoop out flesh. Let cool in refrigerator, then mix with all remaining ingredients, except almonds, in blender or food processor. Blend and serve in parfait glasses, topped with almonds.

Note: acorn or butternut squash may also be used for this dish.

Per Serving: 23 Chol (mg); 16 Carbo (g); 3 Prot (g); 25 Na (mg)
Dietary Fiber: 4.5g **Fat (g):** 1; Sat .4; Poly .2; Mono .6 **Calories:** 80
Exchanges: 1 starch/bread

Cool Carob Pudding

Serves: 4
Cooking time: 3 to 4 minutes
Preparation time: 5 minutes plus cooling time

¼ cup unsweetened carob powder (or cocoa)
2 cups evaporated skim milk
1 teaspoon pure vanilla extract
1 teaspoon instant coffee (decaf optional)
1 teaspoon frozen orange juice concentrate
    Filberts, chopped

Combine all ingredients, except nuts, in blender and turn into a 4-cup measure. Cover tightly with vented plastic wrap, and microwave on High for 3 to 4 minutes. Place in freezer for about 1 hour before serving. Stir with fork, spoon into dessert dishes, and top with sprinkle of nuts.

Per Serving: 5 Chol (mg); 18 Carbo (g); 11 Prot (g); 148 Na (mg)
Dietary Fiber: .4g **Fat (g):** 2; Sat .9; Poly .8; Mono .4 **Calories:** 126
Exchanges: 1½ skim milk

Corn and Peanut Pudding

Serves: 4
Cooking time: 7 to 8 minutes
Preparation time: 10 minutes

½ cup canned or frozen corn niblets

1 cup skim milk

1 heaping teaspoon oat bran

1 tablespoon unsweetened coconut, shredded and divided

2 tablespoons frozen orange juice concentrate

1 teaspoon pure vanilla extract

1 teaspoon maple extract

¼ teaspoon ground allspice

½ teaspoon ground ginger

1 tablespoon crunchy peanut butter (no sugar added)

2 tablespoons unsalted peanuts, chopped

Carob chips, unsweetened (available in health food stores)

Microwave corn with liquid on High for 3 minutes. Drain. Turn corn niblets into food processor and puree. Pour in milk and all remaining ingredients except peanuts, carob chips, and half tablespoon of the coconut. Process until smooth.

Pour into 8-inch deep casserole, and microwave uncovered on High for 3 minutes. Stir, and microwave another 1 to 2 minutes, until thick. Let rest a few minutes and top with remaining coconut, peanuts, and carob chips. Serve warm or chilled.

Per Serving: 1 Chol (mg); 14 Carbo (g); 5 Prot (g); 56 Na (mg)
Dietary Fiber: 2.2g **Fat (g):** 4; Sat 1.0; Poly 1.0; Mono 1.6 **Calories:** 103
Exchanges: 1 starch/bread; 1 fat

Couscous Pudding

Serves: 4
Cooking time: 6 to 8 minutes
Preparation time: 5 minutes plus resting time

2 cups skim milk
¾ cup couscous
1 tablespoon currants
½ teaspoon orange zest
½ teaspoon whipped butter
2 teaspoons pure vanilla extract
1 tablespoon almonds, chopped
Few dashes cinnamon
2 strawberries, sliced in half

Pour milk into 6-cup glass measure or casserole, and microwave on High for 2 to 3 minutes, until it boils. Add couscous and remaining ingredients, except almonds, cinnamon and strawberries. Microwave on High for 4 to 5 minutes, until liquid is absorbed. Stir to blend.

Let rest 5 minutes. Spoon into individual dessert glasses, and top with almonds and dash of cinnamon. Garnish with strawberry slice.

Per Serving: 3 Chol (mg); 22 Carbo (g); 8 Prot (g); 73 Na (mg)
Dietary Fiber: .7g **Fat (g):** 2; Sat .4; Poly .2; Mono .6 **Calories:** 132
Exchanges: 1 starch/bread; ½ skim milk

Crème Fraîche

Serves: 10 (2-tablespoon servings)
Cooking time: 1 to 2 minutes
Preparation time: 2 minutes plus standing and chilling time

1 cup part-skim ricotta cheese
¼ cup buttermilk

Whip cheese and buttermilk in blender until smooth. Pour into dish and microwave on High 1 to 2 minutes, until just warm. Let stand a few hours before chilling. Use a dollop over fruit desserts.

Per Serving: 7 Chol (mg); 1 Carbo (g); 3 Prot (g); 32 Na (mg)
Dietary Fiber: 0g **Fat (g):** 2; Sat 1.1; Poly .1; Mono .5 **Calories:** 31
Exchanges: free (limit to 2-tablespoon serving)

Fancy Fruit Soup

Serves: 4
Cooking time: 3 minutes
Preparation time: 5 minutes

- ½ cup dried apricots
- ½ cup Dole's orange-pineapple-banana juice (or orange juice)
- ½ cup prunes, pitted
- 1 cinnamon stick
- 4 whole cloves
- 2 slices lemon
- 2 tablespoons non-fat plain yogurt
- 1 tablespoon pecans, chopped
- 1 teaspoon unsweetened coconut

Place apricots in medium bowl with ½ cup juice and cover with vented plastic wrap. Microwave on High for 1 minute. Add prunes, cinnamon stick, cloves, and lemon and microwave on High for another 2 minutes, until fruit is soft. Remove cloves and cinnamon stick, mix in yogurt, and serve with sprinkling of pecans and coconut if desired. This is even better after chilling overnight.

Per Serving: 0 Chol (mg); 19 Carbo (g); 1 Prot (g); 9 Na (mg)
Dietary Fiber: 4.7g **Fat (g):** 1; Sat .2; Poly .2; Mono .4 **Calories:** 81
Exchanges: 1 fruit

Coffee Flan (Custard)

Serves: 4
Cooking time: 5 minutes
Preparation time: 5 minutes plus chilling time

- 2 eggs, 1 yolk only
- 1 cup undiluted evaporated skim milk
- 1 teaspoon instant coffee (optional)
- ½ teaspoon pure vanilla extract
- Few drops maple flavoring
- 1 tablespoon frozen orange juice concentrate
- 1 tablespoon orange zest, grated
- Cinnamon
- 1 tablespoon sugar-free or raspberry preserves (optional)

Beat eggs well and set aside. Pour milk into 1-quart measuring cup, and microwave on High for 2 minutes, until it boils. Add coffee if desired and stir to mix. Mix with the eggs and remaining ingredients, except preserves.

Turn into 4 custard cups. Microwave at Medium High (70%) for 3 minutes, rotating cups in oven once or twice. Remove and chill in refrigerator. When ready to serve, invert onto a dish and top with dollop of berry preserves.

Per Serving: 71 Chol (mg); 10 Carbo (g); 7 Prot (g); 115 Na (mg)
Dietary Fiber: 0g **Fat (g):** 2; Sat .5; Poly .2; Mono .6 **Calories:** 81
Exchanges: 1 skim milk

Great Grapefruit Bake

Serves: 4
Cooking time: 3 minutes
Preparation time: 5 minutes

> 1 medium grapefruit
> 1 medium navel orange
> 1 tablespoon apricot preserves, no sugar added
> Cinnamon
> 1 tablespoon poppy seeds
> 1 tablespoon walnuts, chopped

Peel and section grapefruit and orange and arrange on serving platter, alternating sections. Dot on apricot preserves and sprinkle generously with cinnamon and poppy seeds. Cover with vented plastic wrap, and microwave on High for 3 minutes. Remove wrap and sprinkle with walnuts. Serve warm or chilled.

Per Serving: 0 Chol (mg); 10 Carbo (g); 1 Prot (g); 8 Na (mg)
Dietary Fiber: 1.4g **Fat (g):** 1; Sat. 1; Poly .6; Mono .2 **Calories:** 46
Exchanges: 1 fruit

Indonesian Pudding

Serves: 4
Cooking time: 6 to 8 minutes
Preparation time: 10 minutes

<pre>
      1 yam (about ¼ pound), peeled and cut into small cubes
      2 tablespoons frozen orange juice concentrate
      1 cinnamon stick
1½ to 2 ripe bananas, peeled and sliced (about 1 cup)
      ½ cup skim milk
      1 tablespoon oat bran
      1 teaspoon pure vanilla extract
        Pinch nutmeg
      6 pecan halves
      1 teaspoon unsweetened coconut, shredded
</pre>

Place yam cubes in 8-cup glass measure with orange juice concentrate and cinnamon stick. Cover with vented plastic wrap, and microwave on High for 4 to 6 minutes, until soft, rotating cup and stirring mid-cycle. Add remaining ingredients, except pecans and coconut, and microwave covered on High for 2 more minutes.

Turn into blender or food processor and whip until smooth. Serve warm (or chill in freezer for 1 hour) in dessert dishes, topped with pecans and sprinkling of coconut.

Per Serving: 5 Chol (mg); 22 Carbo (g); 3 Prot (g); 20 Na (mg)
Dietary Fiber: 2.1g **Fat (g):** 2; Sat .4; Poly .5; Mono 1.1 **Calories:** 109
Exchanges: 1 starch/bread; ½ fruit

Jane's Red Applesauce

Serves: 4
Cooking time: 5 to 6 minutes
Preparation time: 10 minutes plus chilling time

- 3 Golden Delicious apples, cut into eighths
- ½ cup fresh cranberries
- 1 tablespoon frozen orange juice concentrate
- 1 cinnamon stick
- 4 pecan halves

Place all ingredients, except pecans, in a 1-quart measure and cover with well-vented plastic wrap. Microwave on High for 3 minutes. Stir, and microwave on High another 2 to 3 minutes, until apples are soft. Discard cinnamon stick, turn into a food mill, and grind over a bowl. Chill until ready to serve, and top with a few pecans.

Per Serving: 0 Chol (mg); 18 Carbo (g); 1 Prot (g); 0 Na (mg)
Dietary Fiber: 2.6g **Fat (g):** 2; Sat .2; Poly .5; Mono 1.1 **Calories:** 86
Exchanges: 1 fruit

Orange Cheese Cake

Serves: 6
Cooking time: 10 minutes
Preparation time: 15 minutes plus chilling time

> 1 cup part-skim ricotta cheese
> ¼ cup 1% cottage cheese
> 2 eggs, 1 yolk only
> 1 tablespoon pure vanilla extract
> 1 teaspoon maple extract
> Pinch nutmeg
> 1 tablespoon whole wheat pastry flour
> 2 tablespoons frozen orange juice concentrate
> 3 tablespoons orange peel, grated
> 4 tablespoons Grapenuts
> 4 sliced strawberries, blueberries, kiwi, or banana for topping if desired

In a deep bowl, combine first nine ingredients, reserving 1 tablespoon of orange peel. Beat with a hand mixer or use food processor to blend quickly. Turn into a 9-inch quiche or pie dish, and microwave at 80% power for 8 minutes, rotating the dish once. Microwave on High for 2 minutes more. Cake is baked when a knife inserted in center comes out clean.

Dust top with Grapenuts and reserved orange peel. Refrigerate for a few hours, or make this the day prior to serving. Before serving, top with sliced fruit or berries. Lemon juice and lemon rind may be substituted for the orange.

Per Serving: 57 Chol (mg); 10 Carbo, (g); 8 Prot (g); 97 Na (mg)
Dietary Fiber: .7g **Fat (g):** 4; Sat 2.0; Poly .2; Mono 1.2 **Calories:** 101
Exchanges: 1 skim milk; ½ fat

Pink Pear Poach

Serves: 4
Cooking time: 4 minutes
Preparation time: 7 minutes

2	ripe Anjou pears, pared and quartered
¼	cup orange juice
1	slice lemon
1	tablespoon unsweetened cranberry juice
	Dash each of powdered cinnamon and ginger
	Few whole cloves
2 to 3	large ripe strawberries, sliced
1	teaspoon almonds, slivered

Arrange pears in one layer in round 9-inch glass pie plate. Add all ingredients, except almonds, and cover with wax paper. Microwave on High 2 minutes. Turn, re-cover, and microwave on High another 2 minutes. Uncover, discard cloves, and garnish with almonds when ready to serve, warm or chilled.

Per Serving: 0 Chol (mg); 16 Carbo (g); 1 Prot (g); 0 Na (mg)
Dietary Fiber: 2.9g **Fat (g):** 1; Sat .1; Poly .2; Mono .3 **Calories:** 66
Exchanges: 1 fruit

Rice Pudding

Serves: 6
Cooking time: 5 to 7 minutes plus 20 minutes for rice
Preparation time: 15 to 20 minutes

- 1 cup cooked brown rice (use ½ cup brown rice and 2 cups of water. Microwave on High for 20 minutes, stirring)
- 1 large banana, mashed
- ½ cup non-fat dry milk cup water
- 1 teaspoon sesame seeds
- 1½ teaspoons maple extract
- 1 teaspoon ground cinnamon
- Dash ground nutmeg
- ¼ cup frozen orange juice concentrate
- 1 tablespoon raisins
- 2 egg whites, beaten until stiff
- 1 tablespoon sunflower seeds

Mix together all ingredients except last two. Fold egg whites into rice mixture, and turn into 4 x 8-inch loaf pan. Top with sunflower seeds. Place pan on inverted saucer, and microwave on High for 5 to 7 minutes, until set. Serve warm or chilled.

Per Serving: 1 Chol (mg); 23 Carbo (g); 5 Prot (g); 63 Na (mg)
Dietary Fiber: 1.6g **Fat (g):** 1; Sat .2; Poly .6; Mono .2 **Calories:** 121
Exchanges: 1 starch/bread; ½ fruit

Russian Rhubarb

Serves: 4
Cooking time: 6 to 8 minutes
Preparation time: 8 minutes plus resting time

> 1 pound fresh rhubarb, trimmed, cut into 1-inch pieces (about 2 cups)
>
> 1 stick cinnamon
>
> 2 tablespoons frozen orange juice concentrate
>
> 1 cup strawberries, sliced
>
> 1 tablespoon filberts (hazelnuts), chopped

Place rhubarb, cinnamon stick, and orange juice in l-quart glass casserole. Cover with vented plastic wrap, and microwave on High for 3 to 4 minutes. Stir, and microwave on High for another 3 to 4 minutes, covered. When rhubarb is tender, add strawberries and let rest 5 minutes. Discard cinnamon stick before serving, warm or chilled. Serve with sprinkling of filberts.

Per Serving: 0 Chol (mg); 10 Carbo (g); 1 Prot (g); 3 Na (mg)
Dietary Fiber: 2.5g **Fat (g):** 1; Sat. 1; Poly .2; Mono .9 **Calories:** 52
Exchanges: 1 fruit

Spicy Bananas

....

Serves: 4
Cooking time: 1 ½ to 2 minutes
Preparation time: 5 minutes

> 2 small bananas
> 4 tablespoons frozen apple juice concentrate
> ¼ teaspoon ground cinnamon
> ¼ teaspoon ground allspice
>   Dash ground nutmeg
>   Dash ground cloves
> 1 teaspoon sunflower seeds
> 4 strawberries, sliced

Slice bananas into thin rounds and place in bowl with remaining ingredients, except strawberries. Toss gently to coat. Microwave on High for 1 ½ to 2 minutes, until bananas are heated through. Remove to dessert dishes and top with sliced berries.

....

Per Serving: 0 Chol (mg); 18 Carbo (g); 1 Prot (g); 2 Na (mg)
Dietary Fiber: 1.2g **Fat (g):** 0; Sat 0; Poly 0; Mono 0 **Calories:** 72
Exchanges: 1 fruit

Sweet Potato Fruit Bake

Serves: 4
Cooking time: 8 to 9 minutes
Preparation time: 15 minutes

- 1 sweet potato (or yam), peeled and sliced (about 2 cups)
- 2 tablespoons unsweetened pineapple juice
- 1 cup apple, peeled and diced
- ¾ cup unsweetened pineapple tidbits
- 2 tablespoons apricot preserves, no sugar added
- 6 whole cloves
  Few dashes cinnamon
- 1 tablespoon blanched almonds, slivered
- 1 tablespoon unsweetened coconut, shredded

Place sweet potato pieces with pineapple juice in 4-cup glass measure or casserole, and cover with vented plastic wrap. Microwave on High for 5 minutes, turning and stirring once or until potatoes are tender.

Mix apple, pineapple tidbits, apricot preserves, and cloves. Arrange potatoes on 9-inch glass pie plate and top with fruit mixture. Sprinkle with cinnamon. Cover with wax paper, and microwave on High for 3 to 4 minutes. Let cool a few minutes and top with almonds and coconut.

Note: Other fruits such as oranges, kiwis, or berries may be substituted for pineapple tidbits and apples.

Per Serving: 0 Chol (mg); 37 Carbo (g); 2 Prot (g); 26 Na (mg)
Dietary Fiber: 4.3g **Fat (g):** 1; Sat .5; Poly .2; Mono .4 **Calories:** 153
Exchanges: 1½ starch/bread; 1 fruit

Index